write tech

write
tech

How to harness the power
of writing to achieve
audacious goals,
solve any problem,
and radically
re-engineer your life

Jonathan Temporal

Temporal House
books that empower

Published by Temporal House
Sydney, Australia
www.temporalhouse.co

Text and copyright © Jonathan Temporal, 2020

All rights reserved. No part of this publication may be reproduced, distributed, or transmitted in any form or by any means, including photocopying, recording, or other electronic or mechanical methods, without the prior written permission of the publisher, except in the case of brief quotations embodied in critical reviews and certain other non-commercial uses permitted by copyright law.

Title: WriteTech: How to harness the power of writing to achieve audacious goals, solve any problem, and radically re-engineer your life / Jonathan Temporal, author

First Printing, 2020

ISBN: 978-0-646-82610-3 (hardback)

Cover, interior design and typesetting by Florencio Ares

Typeset in Adobe Garamond Pro 12pts.

Printed in the United States of America

I dedicate this book to my family.

For my parents Florentino Garcia Temporal and Corazon Olavides Temporal

> …you both raised me to be the man I am today, loved me unconditionally and always believed in me. Thank you.

For my sister Florence and brother Dennis

> … you have both been among my lifetime mentors; many of the things I have learned from you have found their way in one form or another in the techniques I share in this book. Thank you.

For my partner Antonella Marsili

> …your strength of spirit, compassion, courage and generosity inspire me every day to strive to be the highest version of myself. Thank you.

"Go now, write it on a tablet for them,

inscribe it on a scroll,

that for the days to come

it may be an everlasting witness."

— Isaiah 30: 8

"All I need is a sheet of paper

and something to write with, and then

I can turn the world upside down."

— Friedrich Nietzsche

CONTENTS

Foreword 1

Part One: Discovering a New Way

The Power of the Written Word 9
Why We Write 19

Part Two: The Techniques of WriteTech

Technique One: Mind Your Energy
Writing to control mental focus and direct will power 23

Technique Two: Writing to the 100th Power
Intensified writing for exponential outcomes 35

Technique Three: Life Scripting
Perfect environments and days by design 47

Technique Four: GoalSeek
A powerful goal setting paradigm 67

Technique Five: Gratitude Listing
Create your own miracle in 40 days 83

Technique Six: Superconscious Writing
Downloading from the Universal Supercomputer 105

Technique Seven: Calling S.O.S. to the Universe
When you need to manifest a solution fast 129

Technique Eight: Vision Mapping
Set a course to your true life vision 143

Technique Nine: Think, Write, Decree
The combustible power of decrees 159

Technique Ten: Discernment of the Spirits
A full-proof 400-year-old decision-making technique 171

Technique Eleven: Love letters to and from a future beloved
Call out to your perfect mate using pen and paper 189

Technique Twelve: Creating solid self-confidence
Recall past victories and acknowledge present wins to
create rock hard self-belief 207

Technique Thirteen: Charting Your Hero's Journey
Using clues from patterns of the universal human story to guide your life 223

Part Three: Troubleshooting and FAQs

Appendices 259

Foreword

The dictionary definition of the word 'technology' is 'the practical application of knowledge especially in a particular area', or 'a capability given by the practical application of knowledge'.

By this definition, writing is technology. Denise Schmandt-Besserat, professor emerita of Art and Middle Studies at the University of Texas at Austin, captured the true nature and essence of writing as technology when she wrote: "Writing is humankind's principal technology for collecting, manipulating, storing, retrieving, communicating and disseminating information."

Writing is technology and when we write, we are using possibly one of the earliest, and certainly one of the most important, technologies ever invented. And just as with any technology, writing involves many processes, innumerable techniques. Writing as technology. Writing as a technique. WriteTech. This explains the title of my book.

Writing is ancient. The Sumerians invented writing as a way of recording what they spoke. The ancient Egyptians called writing the 'language of the gods'. The Arabs of old used writing as a tool to elegantly convey ideas. The Roman emperors used writing to proclaim their victories and preserve them forever. At Iona, a remote island off the coast of Scotland, in the 6th century, monks wrote to proclaim and spread Christianity and keep the fire of their faith burning. Today, through the exact same fusion of mind, thoughts, ideas, hand, pen and paper that these ancient peoples employed, we write to convey our joys, triumphs, fears, sadness, grief, despair, hope, faith and gratitude.

Writing is the simplest, most durable and enduring information recording system ever invented. When something is written on a durable medium, whether rock, marble, papyrus, leather or vellum, it endures indefinitely. To this day, we have samples of writing that come from the dawn of human civilization. Unlike information stored in a hard drive, something that is written down on a physical medium doesn't crash, get erased or accidentally deleted. It doesn't need any equipment or other technology to access and read. You simply open the medium it's written on and read.

Writing is powerful. It can communicate a message or an idea that was written thousands of years ago, exactly as it was intended to be understood by the writer. While writing was created principally to be the carrier, the recorder, of spoken language, it is infinitely more powerful than the latter. The ability to speak a language dies with the person; what the person wrote, however, endures past death. Writing can solve your most perplexing problems. Several techniques taught in this book, in particular in Chapters 1, 2, 6 and 10, will show you how to turn your brain into the most fantastic problem-solving machine; writing is the mechanism that directs that machine.

Writing clarifies. The human mind is the most powerful machine in all of creation: properly directed, it can solve any problem. But if left undirected, it also has the destructive capacity to run like an unhinged freight train. Experts estimate that the average human brain thinks 50,000 thoughts in a day, with some experts even saying that number could be as high as 80,000. That's a lot of thoughts – about 3,000 thoughts per hour, 50 thoughts per minute, and 1 thought per second. And the majority of those thoughts –

up to 70% – are negative. Writing is a potent tool to rein in your mind and direct your thoughts only toward desirable outcomes. In Chapter 1, I'll teach you some powerful techniques to do this.

Writing is magical. It transcends time and space. It connects humans in the deepest of ways that no other technology invented can do. Provided we have the ability or the means to understand it, we can read something that was written in a dead language in eons past, and immediately understand what the writer wished to convey at the moment of writing. And with the addition of thought, imagination and emotion, we can also feel exactly what the writer felt at the time of writing.

Writing is the most wonderful time machine ever invented. It can take you back to your past and your future. It can record the minutest details of an experience. Write something, read it back many years later and find yourself transported back to the moment described in your words.

Through writing, you can create your future. In this book, you will learn several amazing techniques to do exactly that. You can describe in vivid detail what you would like to happen a month or a year from now, and forget about what you wrote. Then a month or a year on, you read back what you wrote and you are surprised by the eerie feeling that what you described in the past has come to pass in the future.

This leads me to the last, and most amazing, virtue of writing. Writing is creative. And I don't mean that we can creatively communicate through our writing. I don't mean creating stories either. *Writing creates.* I believe the German Philosopher Friedrich Nietzsche was alluding to this attribute of writing when he said, "all I need is a sheet of paper and something to write with, and then I can turn the world upside down."

Writing can literally create reality – we can shape reality through writing, use it to weave the very fabric of creation – time and space – and to bring into existence circumstances, experiences and conditions that we desire. In short, through writing, we can transform our world and what we perceive as reality.

This book is all about the creative power and magic of writing. It was borne of the desire to share my experiences of the majesty of the power of writing, how I have used and continue to use it to shape my life, and to teach what I have learned to help others do the same. The WriteTech techniques described in this book comprise the cheapest life-altering and life-shaping technology ever created because all you need to start is a pen, a notebook and an optional pocket notebook. You could even use plain sheets of white paper. Ultimately, it doesn't matter what medium you use; what is important is that you write. So, from here on out, always keep a pen and paper handy wherever you are.

The 13 writing techniques that I share in this book are the same ones that were taught to me by various masters and that I have refined and personally used with tremendous and, in several cases, miraculous results. Use one, some or all of them; experiment on them; modify them to suit your own needs; each one holds great potential to change your life. But the power within each technique will remain dormant until you try it yourself. This is why each chapter of this book contains a section explaining in detail how you can immediately try the technique.

People have always sought answers to questions in life. But as time has gone by, people have not necessarily become better at getting authentic answers to the most critical questions. Today people are more confused than at any point in history. This is because we are constantly bombarded with so much information, from so many sources—the mainstream media, the internet, social media, email alerts, instant text messaging—that it's almost impossible to turn it all off. So many people are trying to give us advice, whether solicited or unsolicited—well meaning family and friends, work mates, especially gurus who claim exclusive possession of just the very thing that would solve all our problems if we subscribe to their latest program—that it's almost impossible to separate the wheat from the chaff.

We cannot find authentic answers from other people or from anything outside of us. It's time to start turning within, instead of without. One of the reasons why I wrote WriteTech is to encourage people to seek their own counsel. I hope to urge you, from now on, to start paying less attention to what others around you are saying, and significantly more attention to the quiet, inner voice speaking within. You can hear what it's saying anytime if you know how to tune into it. Your writing will bring out its counsel; it will help you record and understand it and take action based on its guidance.

No matter the goal, regardless of the problem, and irrespective of the change sought, the answer lies in writing, in your writing. My sincerest hope in writing this book is that you learn from these writing techniques and use them to find your own answers. But above all, I hope this book encourages you, simply, to write. May your writing remind you of the tremendous power you hold in your hands in the form of thoughts, words, pen and paper.

Jonathan Temporal
Sydney, Australia
September 2020

Part One:
Discovering a new way

The Power of the Written Word

This is my story of writing. It is the story of my love affair with writing. Everything that follows is an actual, true and verifiable account of how writing has achieved the things I claim in the title of this book.

I still remember the feeling to this day. It was mid-2005. I was 31 years old, an associate lawyer in a well-known and reputable law firm in Manila. I was standing inside the carriage of the light rail train that travelled over the city's major highway. I was doing the regular commute to my office, which was really just a 20-minute drive from where I lived.

I was crammed, body to body, with a carriage full of strangers. Talk about breathing on other people's necks. I felt stuck.

I stared at the traffic below. If you've been to any major Southeast Asian capital city and driven or commuted during peak hours, then the term "rush hour traffic" would very likely have already taken on a completely new, visceral meaning for you. Venturing into Manila rush hour traffic is an adventure into the unknown. Imagine perhaps fifty thousand cars crammed within a four-lane, 24 kilometer stretch of highway, all travelling southward, and needing to arrive at essentially the same destinations by 9 a.m. You get the picture. When I was child growing up in Manila, my family and I would ride in our car on weekends and travel outside the city. We would breeze through this same stretch of highway that

I was on that morning; it was normal for us to reach our destination within half an hour. But this was many years later. Two to three-hour trawls through morning traffic had become my new "normal".

I stared at the cars and felt sorry for the drivers. They're stuck too, I thought. Just as stuck as everyone around me in the train carriage was. Just as stuck as I was. In truth, I'd been feeling stuck in almost every conceivable sense for a long time prior to that early morning commute to work.

I had already started my professional life as a lawyer. I was on track to reaching all the major milestones I had targeted when I graduated from college. At 21, I was starting at one of the best law schools in the land. At 25, I was editor-in-chief of the law review, and set to graduate, armed with a job offer from the richest, most prestigious law firm in the country. Six years later, I was a promising young associate attorney, on the fast track to make partner one day. I had not yet reached the summit of the mountain where every lawyer one day aspired to sit, but I was well on the way.

As I stood inside that packed commuter train that morning, however, looking down at the cars crammed like matchboxes, a deep and quiet uneasiness gnawed at my insides. It was a feeling I had become all too familiar with in recent months. It was a feeling that I was finding increasingly hard to deny or justify, and even harder to run or hide from.

I was miserable. Not because my life was bad – as you can expect, it was far from that – but because I knew I was meant to do something else and be someplace else. I was miserable because, as I looked at the endless stretch of highway below me, with thousands of hot and sweaty, impatient and unhappy drivers, perhaps most of them only being forced, like me, to go wherever it was they were driving to, I saw that this would be my life for the next 30 years. A life of dreary rush hour commutes, unceasing work pressure, stuffy, conservative meetings, and working for money in a job that I was not passionate about. A life that was as far away, both in time and space, from the life that I knew, down to my core, I was meant to be living.

This was the exact moment that I heard the call to adventure. In the final chapter of this book, I describe the call to adventure that precedes every "hero's journey" that many of us will hear in the course of a lifetime. It is the call to venture forth into an unknown, mysterious future, where nothing is promised or certain. But it is a call that we must heed if we are to have a chance of experiencing the fullness of life that awaits all heroes who go on the quest.

I had heard the call once or twice before, but I closed my ears to it because otherwise it would mean quitting my profession. And I was never a quitter. How could I possibly explain this to my family, especially to my mother? She'd worked so hard to put me through almost five years of law school after my father died when I was 21. Now that she had every reason to anticipate some reasonable return on the investment in me, how could I tell her I was leaving a well-paid, secure job in a prestigious law firm, and leaving the profession that she and my father had dreamed I would one day be successful in?

I had reached the office tower where my law firm occupied two whole floors. I was still unnerved by the experience in the train of hearing the call. It still whispered so loudly in my ears as I was entering the posh, air-conditioned lobby. I stared at the listless expressions on the faces of the yuppies going in and out of the gleaming, polished sliding doors. As I approached those doors, I saw my own face reflected on their shiny, mirror-like surface. Horrified, I realized that my eyes looked lifeless. Suddenly, I knew that I couldn't deny the call to adventure, not this time. If I did, I was in danger of losing myself and ending up just like those elegantly-dressed corporate zombies walking through the glass doors. Again, the call resounded in my ears; only this time, it was no longer whispering. It was blaring.

When that happened, I knew my life, as I knew it, was over. That call had gripped me by the neck and was not going to let go. But I didn't know what or where I was being called to. I knew I needed to go on my own journey, but I was clueless where to start. I was going to leave everything behind—my family, friends, job, and possibly even my home and country—but I didn't know what, if anything, I would gain in return. I needed guidance. I needed answers to the countless questions racing through my mind. I needed encouragement and assurance that I was doing the right thing. But above all, I needed to develop the strength and the faith to do what was required next. I turned to the only dependable, solid thing that had saved me in similar situations in the past. I turned to my writing.

We unleash a tremendous dormant creative force every time we write with serious, deliberate intent. This is a principle that has guided me and I've taken advantage of my whole life.

I first learned this when I was about nine or ten years old. My mother had been taking me and my siblings along to attend regular Science of the Mind and Man seminars led by this alluring, mysterious and inexplicably charismatic lady called Charley. At that time, Science of the Mind was a new thing and Charley was the only person around who taught it. And she taught it like no one else I had seen before or since.

Her seminars were packed. There was an energy about this woman, with her commanding stature, her full-bodied flaming auburn hair, face made-up like the Egyptian Queen Nefertiti, which

The Power of the Written Word

enthralled an entire roomful of grown, smart, sensible and rationally-minded adults. I still remember my mother, and her friends whom she regularly managed to bring to those seminars, hanging on to Charley's every word as she delivered her nightly lecture on strange, mystical concepts like mind energy, the collective unconscious, positive thinking, symbiotic energy fields, affirmations, and many others. The adults were captivated.

And how did her talks affect me? Well, I was a young, impressionable boy at the time. I didn't stand a chance. This woman had smitten me with her unearthly ideas and I was beyond salvation. And I was only 10 years old! If she had looked me straight in the eyes and told me in her calm, low and slightly husky voice to shave my head and become a Buddhist monk, I probably would have.

One thing Charley taught was that each person could "think and decree" things into reality. To decree is to state that something is so and laying it down as law that must be obeyed. Charley taught that if you desire something, you think about it and write a decree. I always asked my mother who was going to read this decree and obey it, and she explained that it was God.

Every night after each seminar, tables set up outside the exits of the seminar room offered up an array of products that could be of interest to Charley's students. Books were commonly sold, as were trinkets, amulets and various stones and crystals. But what always caught my attention were these small, bright green notebooks called "Think and Decree" notebooks. I knew they were called that only because those were the words printed in small, light colored font on the top of each blank page of the notebook. I liked them because they were curious objects – empty notebooks that held the promise that you would get whatever you asked for if you wrote it on those pages.

You can just imagine how enticing these "Think and Decree" notebooks were for a kid. I wrote everything I wanted to have – a new BMX bike, an ATARI video game console (yes this was way before PlayStation), a complete set of Hardy Boys books, etc. I asked solely for material things—hey I was a kid! I was sure I would get whatever I listed down in the Think and Decree notebook, even completely frivolous things like my own basketball ring, because, honestly, I thought it was a Christmas list that my parents would eventually sneak a peek at.

I would eventually learn that the point of these Think and Decree notebooks was not to use them like a Christmas present wish list. I would also soon realize that I did not actually get every single thing I wrote on there. I got only those things that I truly and deeply desired, which I thought about most of the time, and that I wrote down and absolutely expected to get.

So, I did get many things that I listed down in my Think and Decree notebook. At first, I thought that it was the notebook itself that was special, that Charley must have imbued it with some of her mystical mojo. But eventually I realized that the notebook was only a tool, and that it was not the tool that was anything special or carried magical powers. It was what I did with that tool that carried, or more appropriately, activated the magical power. And it was this power (which I would also quickly learn was not my parents!) that brought me what I wrote down.

As early as then, I was being taught a priceless lesson by this simplest of tools – a small blank notebook – that whatever I truly desired and wrote down with deliberate intent, which I believed, with a simple, child-like faith I would get and took inspired action to get, would eventually become mine. I learned this lesson at 11 years old, and it would be my rock, my anchor growing up. It is the same principle that powers each technique in this book.

Having been introduced to the concept of using writing as a transformative and creative tool, it was no longer an alien idea to me by the time I found myself stuck in the light rail train carriage with a hundred other passengers. But after practicing writing in this way as a boy, I had never again written a goal in a Think and Decree notebook or any other notebook.

How often in your life have you learned something valuable—a piece of knowledge, principle or skill—that had the power to elevate you to a higher level and transform you into the best and most amazing version of yourself? And how many times did you learn that valuable principle or skill and never applied or practiced it ever again?

Well I had been taught something powerful and amazing in writing a goal down on paper and decreeing it so. But I never practiced it again. This was unusual considering that writing was in my soul. I had started keeping a journal, in which I consistently wrote, since I was 16 years old. I loved to write. I needed to write. Writing for me is as essential as thinking and breathing.

Soon after that light rail experience, I was browsing through a bookstore when I saw a book that I felt had been written just for me. It was *Write It Down, Make It Happen* by Henriette Klauser. The book explained how simply writing your goals in life was the first step to achieving them. Henriette explained the science behind how and why writing things down tends to actualize what has been written. In the book were collected the stories of ordinary people who witnessed miracles large and small unfold in their lives after they performed the simple act of writing their dreams on paper.

The book was the wake-up call that I had been waiting for. In chapter 13, *Charting Your Hero's Journey*, I write how the call to adventure is often accompanied by a herald. It is as if the universe knows we are ready for adventure and sends us a sign—it could be a person, event, circumstance that tells us we are on the right track, that we should go on an adventure. The sign could be literally anything. Even a book.

Write It Down, Make It Happen contained stories of people who had heard their own calls to adventure in the form of a strong desire to do something that they had never done before, a dream or ambition that was seemingly irresponsible or even crazy to the world. But it was something that they knew they had to do or they would forever exist unfulfilled, living half-lives.

One story in particular was about a theater usher on Broadway who hatched a crazy dream to be an opera singer and go live in Italy to learn the language of opera. He wrote down a goal to live in Italy for a month and learn Italian. As soon as he wrote down that clearly defined goal on paper, his heart skipped. He knew that this was something he needed to do at that exact moment in his life.

This story and every other story in the book reminded me of something I already knew since I had listened to Charley's lectures as a boy and bought one of her magical green "Think and Decree" notebooks; it was something that I had once learned but since forgotten. Since I could no longer get hold of the original "Think and Decree" notebook and Charley had since disappeared, I bought a similar small green notebook. I wrote "Think and Decree" on the cover page as well as the top of every page, just like the original notebook. On May 16, 2006 I wrote one of the first entries in that notebook:

> *I want to work, live, build and establish ties in Australia. I want to experience life there for an extended, indefinite period of time and I want this to happen by January 2007, when I'm 33 years old.*

I wrote down this goal when I was 32 years old. When I wrote it, I had no idea how I could accomplish it. I had neither plan nor resources to achieve it. I was totally clueless as to how I could pull off the massive job of packing up and leaving family, job, friends and home to go live in a country I had never been to, for what could be forever. Still, that was what I wanted and I wrote it down. But miraculously, exactly 5 months and 6 days from the time I put down that goal on paper, I landed in Melbourne, Australia. I had started a chain of unusual, extraordinary circumstances all through my writing.

As I write these words, I have been working, living, building and establishing ties in Australia for 13 years and 11 months and counting. I have experienced life here and had countless amazing experiences. I went back to school, met a wonderful woman, built a loving home with her, and started my own publishing company.

I also wrote a book about how I used writing to get what I wanted and take me where I am now. It's the book that you're holding in your hands right now. I wrote it to show you, if you've never heard of the concept before, that writing can help you achieve audacious goals, solve any problem, and radically re-engineer your life, exactly as promised in the title. This book will show you exactly how to do it. And if you've already heard that writing can do all these amazing things, but for some reason you haven't yet brought pen to paper to unleash the true power of writing, then I hope this book encourages you to do just that. All the amazing things that writing can bring you lie waiting. The only thing that you have to do is start writing.

I have deep faith in my life and I truly believe in synchronicity. I know there are no accidents in life. There is a good reason at this exact moment why you are here, holding this book and reading these words. The wisdom contained in this book will answer many questions you've been asking for a long time. I hope you follow the synchronicity that led you here and connected us.

So, let's write.

Why We Write

Principally, we write to chronicle—to record information, events and circumstances so that we can remember and communicate them to others. But apart from this, there are other reasons, too, why we write, why we should write. We can write for three other important reasons: to co-create, receive answers, help and guidance, and inspire ourselves and others.

The 13 techniques described in WriteTech fall under each of the above categories or reasons for why we write.

Under Writing to Co-create are the following techniques:

Writing to the 100th Power (chapter 2)

Life scripting (chapter 3)

GoalSeek (chapter 4)

Love letters to and from a future beloved (chapter 11)

Writing to Receive Answers has the following techniques:

Mind your energy (chapter 1)

Superconscious Writing (chapter 6)

Calling S.O.S. to the Universe (chapter 7)

Discernment of the Spirits (chapter 10)

The following techniques are all under Writing to Inspire:

Gratitude Listing (chapter 5)

Vision Mapping (chapter 8)

Think, Write, Decree (chapter 9)

And Writing to Chronicle will teach the following techniques:

Creating solid self-confidence (chapter 12)

Charting Your Hero's Journey (chapter 13)

I am thrilled at the thought of all the fabulous things that will happen in your life, the grand goals you will achieve, and the wonderful people you'll meet and places you'll visit as you apply these techniques. Like new friends, you'll meet each technique, learn each of their subtle nuances, and discover what makes each one of them special. I am sure you'll grow comfortable with some of them really quickly, while others will take time to familiarize yourself with.

I invite you to share your stories with me so I can, with your permission, share them with the world. Feel free to email me at Jonathan@writetech.co. If I collect enough stories, it might even make for a good sequel to WriteTech! Actually, allow me to write and decree the goal of successfully launching a sequel to WriteTech right now…

Part Two:
The Techniques of WriteTech

Technique One:
Mind Your Energy

Writing to control mental focus and direct will power

I have been a student of the Japanese Martial Art of Aikido for 30 years, starting in high school, and I also taught it for 13 of those years. I have attained the level of 4th degree blackbelt in the art. Translated from the original Japanese, "Ai" means harmony, "Ki" means energy or life-force, and "Do" means the way or path. So Aikido means "the way to union with energy".

One of the many valuable lessons I learned in Aikido is learning how to use my mind to increase physiological awareness and manage energy. Aikido teaches that it's important to constantly monitor awareness and manage energy because the degree to which we are successful in doing these things can largely determine how healthy we feel mentally and physically. Science has now proven that the level of a person's energy has a direct impact on their level of health. Typically, when we are low on energy, we feel down and even depressed, and when we are in this state, we are more prone to become sick. Some disorders are known as "psychosomatic", which means that these disorders, stomach ulcers for example, are caused or aggravated by psychological factors such as stress.

On the other hand, when our energy is high (or in Aikido terms, "strongly extended forward"), then we feel happy, light and upbeat. When we are in this state, we feel active and healthy, and so are less prone to being sick.

If we can be aware that something is going on inside us on a psychological level, for instance, that we are feeling mentally depressed or stressed, it's a sure symptom that our energy is very low. In this case, we might want to elevate our energy so we can correct this situation and stop ourselves from feeling more depressed or stressed out, which as mentioned above, can lead to further physical disorders.

Aikido is brilliant in teaching techniques that allow you to instantly increase your awareness and boost your mental energy. One of these techniques is a simple process called "focusing on your one point". When you start to feel stressed, worried, anxious or afraid, and falling "out of balance", stand straight, relax your body, and take several deep breaths. Then take your mind completely off whatever it is that's causing you to feel stressed, worried, anxious or afraid; instead, focus it on a point located roughly two centimeters, or about the thickness of your fore and middle fingers, below your belly button. This point, which Aikido and Zen meditation call the "one point" is where mind and body meet. By simply bringing your mind to think about this point, excluding all other thoughts, an amazing thing happens. Your body starts to relax and your breathing starts becoming calm. After just a few seconds of thinking of the one point, you are no longer stressed and again feel "balanced".

American self-development guru and motivation expert Tony Robbins also emphasizes the importance of managing our energy levels and to constantly keep them running high. The reason simply being that to be able to go after any big, worthwhile goal – be it excelling in your career, growing your business, finishing graduate school or a degree, getting out of debt, raising your children, or overcoming a bad habit – you need loads of strong, positive energy. The kind of energy that makes you jump out of bed every morning and powers you to achieve goals.

Both Aikido and Neuro-linguistic programming or NLP (which Tony Robbins trained in) teach that whatever you focus on mentally will grow in your mind. If you are faced with a big problem and instead of trying to come up with a solution, all you do is obsess about it, cry and ask, 'why did this happen to me?' then the problem will grow. And if you don't stifle its growth, soon the problem will grow to such an extent that you will reach the state known as 'overwhelm' – when you feel utterly powerless to deal with the problem.

Change your focus, control your outcome

There is an expression that says, "energy flows where attention goes". Have you ever thought about how you immediately feel after receiving good news? As the implications of the good news start to sink in and you go over all the delightful possibilities, you feel excited and alive, like you're on top of the world. Compare this with how you feel right after receiving bad news. As you start mulling over all the horrible implications of the news, then you start panicking, feeling down and hopeless. Either way, the direction of your thoughts produced the feelings.

The same thing happens when you entertain strong, positive, hopeful thoughts or fearful, negative, despairing thoughts about the future. One of the principles Aikido teaches is that "mind moves the body". Similarly, NLP teaches that when you want to alter your physical state of being, for instance, boredom or depression, you simply change your mental focus. In my own experience, whenever

I think about something that I'm afraid will happen in the future, there is an instantaneous negative reaction inside me. I feel terrible inside. Not only that, I feel something bad physically as well. My heart starts racing, my breathing becomes labored and a knot forms in my stomach. And I know that continuing to feel this way, continuing to feel bad about a future event that may or may not happen, is a terrible place to be in. Surely it is not good for my mind and body to be in this state.

On the other hand, whenever I think about my goals, big things I want to accomplish, or my plans for the future, and how bright my future will be if I achieve those goals and succeed in those plans, there is an immediate positive reaction and I feel awesome inside. Physically, too, I feel great and full of energy. I know that if I sustain this feeling, this state, and keep on feeling excited and full of hope for the future, then good things will happen. It's a good place to be in.

"Energy flows where attention goes". Noted NLP practitioner and trainer Dr Tad James wrote that the focus of our thoughts makes a big difference in our results. Our focus is composed of the images we hold in our minds, as well as a myriad other sensations – the sounds we hear, the feelings we feel when thinking about a specific thought, the smells and tastes we experience, and our self-talk. James also emphasized that our commitment for our own good must be to direct our focus so that it is only on what we want and desire.

So, it's critical that we pay attention to what is going on internally. If you are feeling bad, it means that you are paying attention to what you don't want to happen; but if you are feeling great, it's a sure sign that you are dwelling on what you desire. Focus on what you want, not what you don't want. We need to consciously decide moment after moment and to use our will to control the direction of our entire focus – the pictures, sounds, tastes, smells, feelings and self-talk – only toward what we want, not on what we don't want.

I know it's easier said than done. Each one of us, on average, thinks of 3,000 thoughts per hour. How do you even begin to attempt to control such a large volume of thoughts?

Use writing to manage focus and control energy

You don't have to study Aikido or NLP, however, to be able to learn how to shift your focus. You can use your writing to do it. Writing is a powerful way of practicing awareness and controlling your focus. Writing has an amazing attribute, which I believe is unique among human activities. It is the only activity that requires the mind and body to be absolutely and completely synchronized to be done. In other words, when you write something, you have to simultaneously and continuously be thinking of what you are writing about. Try this quick test: write about how much you enjoyed an experience (for example, eating your favorite meal or seeing a breathtaking sight). And while your hand is mechanically writing the words describing how awesome and fantastic and pleasurable the experience was, try to simultaneously think about everything terrible you can about that same experience. Go ahead try it. Or try to think about anything bad, horrible or painful for that matter. You can't because it's impossible. It's because your writing is your thoughts externalized. That's why you can't feel good inside and be writing "I feel terrible". You could probably do this for a few moments, but if you keep writing "I feel terrible" then I guarantee that you will end up actually feeling terrible.

It works in reverse too: if you write and describe a particular feeling (for example "I feel great!") even if you're not feeling that way at that exact moment, or you're not feeling anything specific, but you continue to write the descriptive words, in seconds, you will actually feel what you are writing. Only writing has this ability to command the complete attention of both body and mind. Think about it – you can be cooking (or at least trying to cook) something delicious and be thinking about how bad your day is going; you can be driving on a beautiful mountain road and feel horrible because you're thinking about an unpleasant incident from the other day. You can even be physically doing the two most pleasurable activities for humans – eating and sex – and hold negative, terrible thoughts in your head.

So, I will modify the statement I wrote above. "Energy follows where writing goes." There is tremendous energy behind your thoughts. And it is incumbent upon you, if you want to control your outcomes, to focus this energy and will it only toward your desired outcomes. Earlier, I wrote that one of Aikido's main tenets is that "mind moves the body". But it is equally true that "body moves the mind". The mere act of moving your body, in particular, your hand as it writes down words, can and does move your mind.

You might be asking at this point, "so are you suggesting that every time I start thinking about bad, negative thoughts or start worrying and feeling scared about the future that I write about the opposite?" Yes, that is exactly what I'm suggesting. No that's not right – that's what I am *explicitly* saying you should do. How much do you want whatever it is that you desire? If I told you that the price is to continuously write about it day after day for as long as it takes to achieve that desire, so that you keep your focus only on that and nothing else, would you pay the price?

5 powerful questions that can shift your focus instantly

I credit Tony Robbins and his audio program *Personal Power II* for this technique. To avoid the state of 'overwhelm' I've described above, when you are faced with any problem, ask yourself these 5 questions below.

1. What's great about this? or What's good about this? (If your brain says, "nothing" then ask "What could be great about this?")

2. What's not perfect yet? (presupposing it's going to be perfect)

3. What am I willing to do to make it the way I want it?

4. What am I willing to no longer do in order to make things the way I want them?

5. How can I do what's necessary to get this job done and enjoy the process?

To apply this technique, pull a problem out of your life, something that's a real tough challenge right now. Ask each question in turn and write down the answers. No, it's not enough to just answer them verbally in your head. You have to write your answers on paper so that they come from your brain and are recorded on paper. Remember that the brain is the most amazing computer ever created. It likes to solve problems. But to use it optimally, you have to give it the right tools and writing is one of the best tools to help your brain think of and process information. Writing has the wonderful ability to clarify thoughts. Earlier, I wrote that the human mind can think of anywhere from 50,000 to 80,000 thoughts a day, or about 3,000 thoughts per hour, 50 per minute and 1 per second. If you simply ask one of the 5 questions and answer it mentally, then you add to the plethora of thoughts already swimming around in your mind. I don't know about you, but I already get confused thinking 3,000 thoughts per hour, I don't need to add anymore!

Thoughts are also like links in a never-ending chain. If you don't control them, one thought will link to another and to another and another, and before you know it, you are overwhelmed by this massive chain of thoughts, most of them negative. The human brain can solve any problem, but to be able to do so, it must go to problem-solving mode, instead of problem-dwelling mode. And if we dwell on a problem, rather than the solution, we keep the brain in problem-dwelling, rather than problem-solving mode. The first step for the brain to go into problem-solving mode is to shift focus from what is bad or negative about the situation, to what is good or even great about it. Writing forces our brains to shift from thinking that this problem is hopeless or "unsolvable", to believing that this problem is a challenge, that it is "solvable".

By writing down the answers to the 5 questions, we remove those thoughts from our brains and keep them separate on paper. If we keep them stuck in our heads, other negative thoughts are free to "link" to whatever answer we've created, usually in the form of objections – "ifs" and "buts" – and rationalizations as to why our proposed solution will not work. On paper, our thoughts can remain objective, in black and white as it were, a stark reminder to us that our problem has a solution.

There is another more critical reason, however, why you have to write down your answers to the 5 questions. Writing activates your entire mind and body and forces it to come up with an answer to even the most vexing problems. Brian Tracy, in his book *Goals!* explains that writing is a psychoneuromotor activity. That's a pretty big word that simply means that when you write anything down, you activate your intelligence (mind), emotions (heart) and your physical body too. In other words, through writing, you can involve your entire being and bring it to bear on whatever it is you are thinking about. So, whatever you write down, whether it's a description of how big and unsolvable your problem is or an explanation of how your problem can be solved, gets internalized in your mind, body and heart—in your entire being.

Solving problems, especially big, tricky ones, sometimes calls for more than logic and the intellectual powers of the brain. Sometimes, we need to activate our emotions and our physical bodies as well. Jack Canfield in his book *The Success Principles* teaches that the human body actually intuitively knows the answer to any question that we can ask of it. He describes a strange, yet amazingly accurate method, called "calibration" where we ask questions of our bodies and calibrate our bodies to accurately answer either "yes" or "no" to a question. And as for the heart (emotions), it is wiser than we give it credit. How many times have you been faced with a problem, and thought of a possible solution that seems logically the best option on paper, but something about it just felt wrong? You decide on another option, following your emotions in the process and find out later on that the logical solution would have landed you in even more trouble. Many times, the heart sees through the cold logic of the brain to lead us to the right answers.

By writing down the answers to the 5 questions, we activate our visual, auditory and kinesthetic senses. That's a lot of power being brought to bear on a problem. Moreover, as I will explain in *Chapter 6 Superconscious Writing*, by writing down on paper:

- what's good or even great about a problematic situation

- what you are willing to do to shift the situation to being an ideal one, and

- how you can do what's necessary to solve the problem and even have fun in the process

you program your subconscious mind to think of nothing else but the solutions to your problem.

The conscious mind is powerful, but it shuts off when you sleep. On the other hand, the subconscious mind works 24/7, and continues to whirr like the powerful microprocessor of an advanced supercomputer, even when you are asleep. When you ask the 5 questions and write down any answers that come to you, you are impressing the subconscious mind; without your awareness, the subconscious mind goes to work to bring even more solutions to your problem. After some time asking these questions and writing down and dwelling on the answers, in the end you'll find that not only will you have completely solved your problem, but you may have also created totally new opportunities and had more fun in the process!

Try it yourself: Focus Questions Technique

I've found that the 5 powerful questions technique works best when I do it first thing in the morning or just prior to sleep. You can do the same or do it during the day. There really is no right or wrong time or way to do it. But I've also found this technique works best when you ask your questions and write your answers in a relaxed state and environment. I personally do the first step of the technique just after I wake up and am facing myself in the mirror. When I actually hear and see me ask these questions of myself, I feel like I am seeking answers from my higher self, that part of me that surfaces when I am feeling centered, calm and relaxed.

So, wake up an hour before you normally rise or set aside an hour before your normal bedtime. Draw in several, deep calming breaths, inhaling and exhaling deeply each time. Try to clear your mind from any thoughts and just relax. Then ask the first question out loud, loud enough so you can actually hear your voice saying the words. Wait for a few seconds and feel if any answers are forthcoming. If answers do come, in whatever form, write them down on paper. If you sense no answer is coming, then ask the second question and do the same thing. Repeat the same process until you've asked the fifth and last question. Again, there is no right or wrong way to do this. You can adopt this technique and add your own unique twist to it. You might even find, as I have in the many times I've used this technique, that you ask the 5 questions and absolutely nothing comes. You might even find that you go through several days of asking these questions and do not get any answers. Don't worry if either of these things happens. I guarantee you the answers will come somehow, someway during the day or in the next few days. But it's critical that you are ready to write down the answers when they do come. That's why I always keep a pen and one of my own Think & Command notebooks, which fits perfectly in the breast pocket of my jacket or coat, handy. I write down any ideas that come during the day that seems like an answer to any of the 5 questions.

Key points to remember

I've experienced getting totally unexpected answers and during the most ordinary moments. So be open to receiving answers in whatever form they present themselves. They won't always come in the way you anticipate. Sometimes, something that a colleague or friend says to you in passing, or an image or word on a poster on the side of a bus you glance at when you're walking, or a scent you smell or a sound you hear, alerts you to the fact that this is connected to one of the 5 questions you asked. And as always, write down the answers as you receive them. If the answer is calling you to take some kind of action, then you should do it. I've found that I get faster results when I act on the ideas from the answers I've received to my questioning. And in the process of taking action, I get further answers to the 5 questions, I get more clarity on what I should be doing, and then I take further action. It's a virtuous cycle. Eventually, my questions get fully answered and the problems that prompted me to ask my questions to begin with have now been solved.

Technique Two: Writing to the 100th Power

Intensified writing for exponential outcomes

The number 100 is a very powerful number. It's associated with the best of anything in the world – the 100 largest companies, the top 100 restaurants, the 100 greatest musical bands, the 100 books you have to read or the 100 movies you have to see or the 100 places you have to visit before you die, and so on.

If you're good at math, you would know 100 is the percentage basis where the full amount is 100%. When we need to be the best at whatever we are doing, we are told that we need to be "at 100%". In society, when anything reaches 100 – whether it's 100 years for a country or a person, or whether it's 100 episodes of a TV show – it's considered a great milestone.

The number 100 is composed of the number 1 and 0, which occurs twice. On their own, each of these numbers carries great significance, symbolism and power. Number 1 is commonly associated with the pinnacle or the summit of anything, be it success, accomplishment or achievement. On the other hand, the number 0 symbolizes stability, infinity and eternity (0 multiplied by anything becomes a 0). But it can also symbolize a new beginning, a starting point (as evidenced by the countless books with titles starting with "From 0 to" whatever).

The number 100 then can be viewed as a virtually limitless number 1. It's a number bursting with power and potential. Anything multiplied by 100 becomes something immensely more powerful and significant. I would learn this at a critical point in my life several years ago. Back then, I accidentally stumbled upon just how potent the number 100 was when combined with the power of writing.

Permutable goals

The 12-month period from June 2015 to May 2016 was a time of great personal success and culmination, as well as turbulence and uncertainty for me. When I first moved to Sydney after having lived elsewhere in Australia for six years, I set a big goal to again become a lawyer, an Australian lawyer. This was a gargantuan goal, considering that I had neither money nor resources at the time to accomplish it. Yet I was determined to achieve it and I used the powerful process I describe in GoalSeek (Chapter 4) to help me get it.

In July 2015, I finally completed all the requirements needed for me to finally become a lawyer in Australia. After doing the hard yards for two years, studying practically full-time and working part-time, I was finally ready to be admitted into the practice of law in my new home country. Two months later, in August, I stood proudly in the Supreme Court of New South Wales as Chief Justice Tom Bathurst swore me and a hundred other new lawyers into the legal profession. Then, amazingly, two months after that, another big goal that I had listed down – to work in a Sydney law firm – was also accomplished.

Within a month, however, of starting in the new law firm, I found that it was far from what I had envisioned when I first wrote this particular goal down. I was feeling fulfilled and accomplished because I had once again become a lawyer, but things were not panning out in my new workplace. I soon found myself in the most toxic working environment I had ever been in my professional life. After three months, I was all but ready to quit. Instead, I stuck it out because I was stubborn. I also believed, mistakenly as I later realized, that once a goal had been set, it was unchangeable and I was supposed to see the goal through; and to fall short, or quit, so soon after setting that goal, was to fail and lose. I did not want to be a quitter, yet I was also miserable where I was. I wanted to be successful once again as a lawyer, but there was no denying that I hated working in the toxic environment of this law firm. I rationalized to myself, "but you've been successful in big law firms before, and you didn't quit then, so don't quit now!" From then on, every day at work, I always had one foot out the door. I knew I could not last in this situation.

Fortunately, my dilemma was resolved for me as I was fired from the law firm after four months. While I was extremely relieved because a big weight had been instantly removed from my shoulders, I still felt anxious immediately after I was let go. There were bills to pay and no alternative job prospects on my immediate horizon. Amid my mounting concern and anxiety, I turned to the only thing I knew how to do and do well – I wrote.

Writing for 100 days and nights

I soon got tired of stressing out where I would get the money to pay my bills. Instead of writing a goal to get a job quickly, I aimed higher. I made it a goal to buy a house within 100 days from the time I was fired. This was quite a laughable goal to write at the time. In Australia, no bank would lend me money unless I was in a full-time job and had a strong record of savings. After I was let go from the law firm, I had neither of these. While the goal was laughable, it was very significant for me precisely because buying a house required me to have both money and a job. It was virtually impossible to achieve it and this is exactly why I wrote it down. I had already learned that writing can transform reality, and I had proven this in my life multiple times. I was going to prove it again and it didn't matter that there was no visible means for me to achieve this goal.

In R.H. Jarrett's book *It Works!*, he describes an amazingly simple technique to get what you want: write it down on paper, read it three times each day, morning, noon and night, think of what you want as often as possible, and never talk about it to anyone except to the great power within you, which will unfold to your conscious mind the method for its accomplishment. In *Chapter 4 GoalSeek*, I describe this technique and its variations as well as other guidelines and key points to make it even more effective. I took Jarrett's technique a step further by applying a principle that I already knew: writing acts much like a magnifying glass would when used to focus sunlight. As a magnifying glass can channel sunlight to burn on a minute point and set it on fire, so can writing focus our thought, determination and will on a specific objective. So, I decided that I would write out exactly what I wanted—to buy a house within 100 days from the time I became unemployed—for 100 days straight until I got it.

Through my research on the power of writing as a goal setting and achievement tool, I later discovered that many high achievers do the same or something similar too. Brian Tracy in his book *Goals!* teaches a method of writing down a list of your top 10 to 15 most important goals in a notebook every day continuously until things start happening and you start achieving them. Using my magnifying glass principle, I decided to continuously write just this one overriding goal in my journal. I chose to write it for 100 days due to the power and significance of the number 100 discussed earlier.

Technique Two: Writing to the 100th Power

I bought the house exactly as I wrote I would. But I did not accomplish this exactly on the hundredth day. The contract was settled and I officially owned the house about six months after the one hundredth day of writing. But I didn't complain, not at all. This was a successful outcome. I had gotten what I wanted. It didn't really matter that I didn't get it on or before my due date. During the entire nine-month period, I learned other additional, valuable lessons on this focused-writing process, lessons that will certainly serve me well the next time I use it.

How important is it to set a date within which we want to achieve our goal? It is essential. Setting a date within which to achieve a goal is not so much about setting a deadline for yourself or the world, as it is about making a commitment to yourself that you are serious about getting it. When you write down a goal and date stamp it, many times, you will find that a goal was not achieved within your original timeframe. But if you look back on how things developed after you started writing about the goal, you'll clearly see that the necessary steps, circumstances and events all started happening within the timeframe you set. It was only the ultimate result, that is, the materialization of your goal, which took place after your original due date. This is a normal, and even essential, part of the process of realizing that goal.

The very act of repeatedly and consistently writing one specific goal assures that your goal is kept constantly front of mind. As it is always before you, you are always thinking about it and as you do so, you will be prompted or inspired to take certain actions. These will most likely be small steps at first, but which will later become bigger and bigger. In my case, I took small steps—I isolated the areas where I could afford to buy and calculated my maximum budget. I called a good mortgage broker who had been referred to me from a property investing group I had joined. In terms of bigger steps, I took on part-time jobs, which eventually led to an offer for a full-time job. I accepted this offer because I knew that I would be more attractive to banks when it came time for me to borrow money to buy that first property.

I learned that during the 100 days of writing about your goal, when you are inspired to do a certain act or take a certain step, no matter how small or random it seems at the time, you must follow through the action or take the step. You never know where it will lead. Soon, you will realize that these inspired actions, taken together, formed the bridge that allowed you to cross from your starting point straight to your goal.

Try it yourself: Writing to the 100th power technique

Get your notebook or journal, something easily accessible to you at all times. Choose a time that is most suitable for you to write undisturbed for about 15 minutes to half an hour. The two times best suited for this activity are usually at the start of each day and at least 15 minutes before bed time. For the rationale behind these two times and additional guidelines on choosing which one is ideal for you, see the Morning and Evening Pages technique described in *Chapter 6 Superconscious Writing*.

Write down the single, all important goal you want to achieve – something that you desire to be, do or have. You can use the same rules you will learn in the GoalSeek technique in Chapter 4 and write down your goal in the first person, using strong, affirmative and positive words and always in the present tense. Remember always that you are not asking permission from anyone but yourself to be, do, or have whatever it is you desire. So instead of writing, "To do such and such," write "I am doing such and such". Instead of writing, "I want to have" or "I would like to have", write "I now have" or "I now possess".

Technique Two: Writing to the 100th Power

Describe this goal in detail. The more detail you supply, the better. Doing this might take up your entire 15 minutes to half hour of allotted writing time, which is why the 100-day technique in this chapter is best suited for only one specific goal, not many. You might find it effective to write out a scene as if it is happening right now at the present time or in the very recent past, which implies you have already achieved your goal. For example, in my case, I described the feelings I was feeling as though I was touching the walls and the floor of the house I had just bought. Ask yourself, "what is the first thing I would do right after I achieve this goal?" You might answer, for example, that you would call a certain person and talk to him or her about what you've just accomplished. You would then describe that call in your writing.

Along a similar line, you can try an alternative technique from Neuro-linguistic Programming, which will help amplify the power of your description. Ask yourself, "what is the last step to happen that would imply, without a doubt, that my goal has been achieved?" For example, if your goal was to own a certain house, the very last act that would take place showing, without a doubt, that the goal had been achieved is you taking the house keys from your pocket or bag, inserting the key in the front door key hole, turning it, opening the door and entering the house. Imagine that scene and describe it in detail in your writing.

As you write about the act you would immediately do right after you achieved your goal, be sure to include and describe the feelings you would be experiencing. As explained in *Chapter 1 Mind Your Energy*, the very act of describing a feeling in writing produces that feeling. The body moves the mind. In his book *The Law and the Promise*, American author and mystic Neville Goddard described the importance of identifying and internally generating the feeling of the wish fulfilled. He asks, "what would it feel like if my wish were fulfilled right now?" This is the feeling of the wish fulfilled. You don't have to imagine any particular images or scenes taking place in your mind. Simply ask yourself what feelings would you feel the moment you realized that your wish had been fulfilled. It could be peace, ecstasy, immense relief, or a host of other strong feelings. Feel yourself actually experiencing these feelings at the present moment. Then write about it.

Indicate the day on which you are writing. Similar to writing a date in goal listing, you would write that in 100, or 89 or 57 or 28 days, your desired outcome will come to pass or you will achieve your goal. As you write each day, you will do a countdown, for instance, yesterday you would have written, "in 79 days, I will have what I want…"; today, you will write, "in 78 days, I will have what I want…"; and tomorrow, you will write, "in 77 days, I will have what I want…." You might even wish to highlight the numbers of the days as you count them down. It is critical that this countdown should only create in you a heightening feeling of excitement and anticipation. Think of what it felt like when you were a kid and you counted down the days till Christmas. As you counted the days before you went to bed – 12 days! 11 days! 10 days! – before you get to open your presents, your excitement grew and you couldn't wait for the big day to arrive. Or think of counting down the days until your wedding day arrived. As each day passed, your anticipation to be with your beloved grew until you couldn't wait to be married to her or him.

On the other hand, if you find yourself feeling any stress from writing this countdown, if you find that you're becoming increasingly anxious, irritable or fretful in any way as each day passes, then stop writing the countdown of days. This step is meant to increase strong feelings of positive expectation, excitement and anticipation in you, and not make you a nervous wreck! If you do find yourself feeling stressed out or anxious as Day 1 approaches, just relax, go back to contemplating how awesome it would be to finally realize this desire, and write it down. Or reverse engineer your emotional state through your writing. If you find that you are already feeling distressed as the days wind down, just write out and describe the reverse feeling that you would like to experience. You will find that the moment you write out the feelings you wish to feel, those feelings are quickly generated in your body.

Key points to remember

This technique will work just as well for a longer list of goals as it does with a single goal. But it will be even be more powerful if you focus on a single important goal. As explained above, your writing will act as magnifying lens that will concentrate all your mental energy like sunlight and bring it to bear on the accomplishment of a single, overriding objective.

Psychologically as well, this technique works because your brain more than anything else likes to be stimulated with pleasurable sensations; once it experiences a pleasurable sensation, it will keep seeking out its source so that it can experience it again and again. Seeing that important goal coming closer to you is one of the most pleasurable experiences you'll ever have. It is said that sometimes, anticipation of a pleasurable experience is more pleasurable than the actual experience itself. As you start writing down your single goal and describing it in great detail, you begin to activate the feelings of what it would be like to actually accomplish your goal. Moreover, once you start seeing results as you move closer to your goal, you feel even more motivated, prompting you to take even more action toward it. Throughout this 100-day process, you begin to activate the pleasure-seeking mechanism of your brain and it will continue to feed you with energy and motivation to keep taking steps toward the accomplishment of that single important goal.

One final key point: mind your inner state. During the 100-day stretch, when doubt, disbelief, discouragement or impatience start to creep in, write about what you're going through. It is not unusual to experience doubt and disbelief during this long stretch; it is normal to feel discouraged and impatient, especially when you're thinking that all you've been doing is writing and you do not perceive anything happening to indicate that your goal is inching closer. As I explain, however, in *Chapter 5 Gratitude Listing*, you should acknowledge these "negative" feelings for what they are – confirmations that you are human, subject to all the foibles and frailties that human nature is inevitably subjected to. So yes, it's ok to feel negative and down once in a while as you write your way closer to Day 1. What's not ok is to allow these feelings to shake your definite purpose in getting that goal or quash your faith that you will get it to such an extent that you stop writing. This will be detrimental to the achievement of your goal.

Remember, just because nothing seems to be happening on the physical plane or you don't see anything developing does not mean that this is the case.

I recall seeing a video once that all that it takes to crack a seemingly solid rock is by patiently, but consistently tapping it—not hitting or smashing—at strategic points with a hammer. Applying the same pressure, you tap at that rock, hour after hour, day after day. For a time, it will appear as if all that tapping is doing absolutely nothing to the rock; after a thousand taps, it is clear that the rock looks unchanged – on the outside. But what you don't see and have utterly no way of seeing, is that the rock has slowly been cracking on the inside. Every hammer tap you make creates even more cracks; the longer you tap at the rock, the bigger the fissures on the inside grow. It's tempting to stop at the point when five or three taps or even one more tap of that hammer will completely

Technique Two: Writing to the 100th Power

break the rock. So, don't stop tapping away, don't stop writing just because nothing seems to be happening with your goal.

Minding your inner state is especially critical when you reach the last 10 days of writing. This is the crucial home stretch. Regardless of how many times in the past 100 days you felt in doubt or even if you came close to losing faith, ramp up your writing in the last 10 days. Through your writing, describe your heightened sense of anticipation now the finish line is within reach. Recall everything that felt good when you wrote in the past 100 days. Now relive those feelings again in these last 10 days, but this time, feel them more intensely. Feeling a sincere, deep sense of gratitude and giving thanks that what you want will now surely come to pass and writing this is also one good way to spend the homestretch.

After the one hundredth day, you must now take the last and most important step of all in this whole 100-day process. At this point, whether or not your goal has been achieved or what you desire has come to pass, release it. Let it go. Don't refer to or write about it the next day or in the following days. Know that you've done everything there is to do from your end, and there are no more steps to take. Allow those feelings of positive expectation and delicious anticipation to linger in the coming days. Be easy about this process, knowing that what you want is on its way to you. Above all, cultivate your feelings of faith, gratitude and appreciation for what's to come. I guarantee that if you take this last essential step, your dream, your wish will be fulfilled.

Technique Three: Life Scripting

Perfect environments and days by design

In the sub-title of this book, I make the bold claim that you can transform your life through writing. Many techniques taught in this book are aimed at helping you redesign and recreate specific areas or aspects of your life. But the technique described in this chapter is the most encompassing of all the techniques because it involves you writing and describing in advance the exact quality of life you want to have in the future. Life Scripting will show you how you can design your ideal future life by describing in the present two very specific manifestations of that life: first, your ideal environment, and second, your perfect day. The three techniques I will teach in this chapter all build on each other, so I suggest you do them in sequence.

This chapter is all about writing our life scripts. Each one of us is the author of the script we want our lives to follow; each of us is also the director who alone is responsible for staging that script on the grandest stage of all – our own lives.

Many of us, at one point or another, have wished our lives to follow a certain path or lead to an eventual destination. When we were children, we fantasized about growing up to be someone or something someday. Without us realizing it, at that moment, we were scripting our lives. When I was a child, my earliest desire was, like most boys I suspect, to become an astronaut, like Neil Armstrong. Later on, I wanted to be President of the United States (never mind the fact that this was impossible since I wasn't born in America!). And soon after, I dreamed of becoming a lawyer one day, just like my parents.

As a child, at each of these phases, I scripted a scene in my imagination, depicting my most perfect day, in which I would be doing things and spending time the way I would if I were already what I dreamed of becoming. I spent a lot of my time day dreaming about these scenes. As children, we were all experts at day dreaming. From a very young age, many of us were already starting to practice life scripting, or at least the beginnings of it. I bet many of you too mentally wrote your life scripts and played them out in your heads a lot, just like I did. When I imagined these mental scripts of my perfect day, I'd make everything in it exactly the way I wanted it to be—from the room I was in, the people around me, the things I was doing, words I was saying, to the sounds I'd be hearing. It was my script of my perfect day, I was the author and director, and everything that happened that day was just the way I wanted it. I imagined this and it felt awesome!

In a December 2018 article that appeared on *the balance careers* website, Job search expert Alison Doyle wrote that the top 10 kids' dream jobs are: dancer/choreographer; actor; musician; teacher; scientist; athlete; firefighter; detective; writer; and police officer. She also explained that kids typically want these jobs because of the excitement, the fame, or the chance to help other people. If you are among the kids who dreamed about having these jobs when you grew up, then you must have been scripting your ideal day from the time someone asked you, "what do you want to be when you grow up?"

How many of us though actually get to live those perfect days when we grew up as adults? If we didn't drop our childhood dreams, and as adults still want them, are we fulfilling them? If your childhood ambitions naturally changed as you got older, that's different. That's just the natural evolution of your goals. But what if you never stopped dreaming about being the rock star, famous dancer, renowned scientist or celebrated athlete? Did you eventually become any of those people? If not, then you're not alone.

Mental scripting is not just limited to children. Even as adults, many of us at one point or another find ourselves wishing that we could change careers, and be someone or do something completely different. We may have abandoned our childhood dreams, but we now have a new dream—to reinvent ourselves, to follow our passions and our true callings, and do something that fills us with excitement, zest, joy and fulfillment, to make a difference in the world and the lives of other people. At various times when you're at your desk in the office or commuting to work or home, you must have mentally scripted your perfect day, a little slice of your perfect life, just like you did when you were a kid. Let me ask you a question: did your mental script eventually play out in reality? Did you end up living the dream? Again, if the answer is no, then you're not alone.

Have you ever wondered why some of us don't become what we once, whether as kids or adults, imagined ourselves becoming, why the mental scripts of our perfect days never eventually played out in reality? The reason is because we never moved past fantasizing and wishing.

Wishing versus receiving

Napoleon Hill, author of perhaps the most famous self-help book from the 20th century, *Think and Grow Rich*, wrote: "There is a difference between wishing for a thing and being ready to receive it." He also wrote, "No one is ready for a thing until he or she believes he or she can acquire it. The state of mind must be belief, not mere hope or wish."

So yes, we continuously script our lives. But for some of us, the reason why we never get to play out these scripts in reality, why we never end up living the perfect days we imagined, is because we only wished it would happen for us one day. In order for that script to be elevated from the state of wishing for something to happen to believing it will happen, for us to move from day-dreaming to being ready to receive that which we've imagined in our mental scripts, we need to write out that script! Writing a full-fledged description of what you want is one way of saying you believe that it's attainable and you are ready to receive it. The more precise you can be with your description, the readier you will become to actualizing it. Write your mental script in detail – not only depicting your goal, but rehearsing what the particulars of your life will be like once this goal is achieved.

If you want your dream life to happen, you must script it. This is the first step that will remove your daydreams from the realm of wishful thinking and take it to the arena of your life's coming attractions. Describe what a normal day would be like for you if you had already successfully reinvented yourself and become the person you once imagined yourself to be, doing the things such a person would do. If you feel you're not particularly imaginative and are having a hard time imagining, let alone, writing a description of, your perfect day, then keep reading. The exercise described below may help.

Twenty things you enjoy doing

I credit the late Barbara Sher, whose book *Wish Craft*, helped guide me in my own process of life scripting. I've followed Barbara's processes as described in her book and they are life-changing. Some

Technique Three: Life Scripting

of her processes, including the one I'm about to describe here, are the inspirations for the Life Scripting technique I will teach later in this chapter.

In the meantime, let's start the process of life scripting by simply listing down twenty things you enjoy doing. List down whatever comes to mind that causes a reaction in you, which fills you with excitement. Later on, we're going to use the activities as the essential ingredients of your perfect day, so make sure not to miss anything! Designing your life really should be no more complicated than creating your own version of your favorite dish. You get to choose the ingredients that will be in the dish. So naturally, you would only include the things that you like and leave out anything you don't.

So, let's list down 20 things you enjoy doing. Yes, you must come up with 20, that's the only rule. Apart from this, there are no rules. Anything goes in your list—from serious, important stuff like "working for myself, growing my business, or planning my future", to seemingly trivial things like "walking my dog, meditating, sketching people, or cooking". If you list down 19 things and you're struggling to get to number 20, just write anything, even "doing nothing" or "listening to the grandfather clock tick in my living room" is pretty good. The reason why you need to list so many is because this will stretch your imagination and force you to really think about the components of your perfect day. Come on it shouldn't be that hard! After all, these are things you like doing!

Draw a chart, with two columns—a left-hand side vertical column, and a right-hand side horizontal column. On the vertical column, list down the 20 things; there's no need to rank them; it will be impossible to rank them anyway because these are all things you enjoy.

On the horizontal column, write the questions below. You might have to turn your paper landscape style to fit these.

Q1: How long since last done?

Q2: Costs money or free?

Q3: Alone or with someone?

Q4: Planned or spontaneous?

Q5: Work or family related?

Q6: Physical risk?

Q7: What do I like about it?

Q8: Involves mind, body or spirit?

For example:

20 things	Q1	Q2	Q3	Q4	Q5	Q6	Q7	Q8
Name Activity 1 here								
Name Activity 2 here								

These are only suggested categories; you can add any other ones that come to mind. If there is one principle that I hope you learn from this book more than any other, it is this: through your thoughts and writing, you have the power and ability to reshape the world to suit you. In fact, it is your God-given right to do so. As with any of these WriteTech techniques, if you can adopt any of them, improve on them, or tailor them to fit your own needs based on your own insights, go for it!

Technique Three: Life Scripting

After you've filled up your chart, let's quickly debrief this exercise. What did you learn about yourself from the things you like doing? Did you spot any patterns? Do several of these things share one or two aspects in common (for example, a love of travel)? Is there a big disparity between the list of 20 things you enjoy doing and the things that you're currently doing in your day to day life right now? Do you see a gap (wide or small) between the quality of your life now and the life that you'd like to live based on the top things you like doing?

By analyzing the activities you enjoy doing, along with the people, places, and things that are indispensable to these activities, you start getting an idea of your own personal style. People commonly associate the idea of "style" with external expressions: how you dress, the way you decorate your home or flat; the kinds of music, movies and books that you like, and it can even extend to the types of food and restaurants you like. Style is normally thought of as something fun, quirky, unique and individual; but ultimately, it is regarded as something extra, trivial, optional, and dispensable.

But style goes way beyond these external expressions; style is your identity, it is your own unique voice, it is who you are. It is the truest expression of your talent, creativity and imagination, not what you do in your job or for work, but the deepest expression of yourself. It is impossible to completely suppress your style, even though society, our families, friends, peers and social networks tend to suppress aspects of our style when they expect us to behave in certain ways. Our style will ultimately find expression and leave clues behind in many areas, such as, for example, in the things you most enjoy doing. You need to honor this expression and take these clues seriously because they will tell you how to design your perfect life. By knowing and listening to your style, you will be able to script your perfect life environment.

Once again, read over your list of things you most enjoy doing; as you do so, start piecing together your personal style. Taking a good look at your own style can show you many things about who you really are and what you truly want. You get to understand and know yourself more, and doing so will give you a sense of confidence that you did not have before.

Preparing to script your perfect life

Using the information and insights you've gained from the "20 things I enjoy doing" exercise, I'm now going to guide you as you shape time and space to suit your desires and needs.

The first thing we're doing is to get you to design your perfect environment, one that's so ideally suited to you that you become the best version of yourself when you're in it. Your ideal environment is the place where your best talents and gifts can naturally express themselves. Once we've done that, we're going to design your perfect day.

I know you might be rolling your eyes and thinking, "sure I could live in my perfect environment, if I could be the queen or king of my own castle, and not have to cook, clean or wash dishes!" or "sure I'd happily live my perfect day, if I had a spare million dollars!" Many of us allow appearances of our present circumstances or the cold hard facts set by our current responsibilities, incomes and the people we're living with to confine our life scripting. We let the facts tell us what's possible and what's not; we let reality dictate how we should create our environments and live out our days, even though we know desperately that we aspire to and deserve something greater.

Faced by the tyranny of appearances, we stay on wishing about our ideal environments and our perfect days, embarrassed to be dreaming self-indulgent, unrealistic, maybe even selfish dreams.

Technique Three: Life Scripting

"Come on be realistic!" we admonish ourselves. "What does it profit me to wish and daydream? What good is it to imagine?"

And yet imagination is very important. "Your imagination is everything. It is the preview of life's coming attractions," Albert Einstein said. Imagining and scripting your ideal environment and day are essential. When you imagine, you give your mind flight. The great boxer Muhammad Ali said, "the person who has no imagination has no wings." All of us should imagine more and take imagination seriously because it's giving us important clues on how to design our perfect lives. As I'll explain more in *Chapter 6 Superconscious Writing*, your imagination is the means by which you communicate with the Superconscious Mind exactly what it is that you desire. And the Superconscious Mind has the ability to orchestrate events and conditions and to cause the conspiracy of circumstances to bring about your perfect environment and your ideal life. "If you can imagine it, you can achieve it. If you can dream it, you can become it," wrote author William Arthur Ward. The poet Blake also wrote, "What is now proved was once only imagined." So don't knock imagination, for it is the beginning of all creation.

Now let's set your imagination soaring and find out where it takes you.

Try it yourself: Life Scripting 1 – designing your ideal environment

Before we launch into Life Scripting, I'm going to ask you to follow one rule: while we are doing it, suspend your judgment, and ignore appearances. Also, there are no irreconcilable conflicts; if you want to do two things that seem to clash with each other, don't stress. Add them both in. If you love living on a farm but also relish the hustle and bustle of city life, or if you want the freedom to travel the world when you please but you have kids to look after, or you value solitude but don't mind being surrounded by people you love, or if you'd like to pursue two careers, just write both alternatives down. I won't tell you to make a choice. You get to have what you want—all of it.

Now write down your answer to this question: In what imaginary environment would my best self emerge?

In Life Scripting, we will try shaping the world to your needs for a change. Imagine an environment that is perfect for someone with all your present characteristics—a world so tailored to your nature that you'd be at your best in it without changing yourself one bit. Let the environment do all the work for you.

To help you in this exercise, let's define the terms a little bit. "Environment" includes your physical surroundings. So, describe the ideal physical environment in which you will feel free to always function at your very best. Be as detailed as possible and include even trivial details, like colors, sizes and shapes of things. But don't spend too much time on the color of your walls or the climate and the vegetation, unless these are indispensable to your ideal environment. What's more important is in your perfect environment, you want to be surrounded by things, occupying spaces and sensing sensations that excite you and make you feel fully alive.

More than just your physical surroundings, however, your environment means your human environment: the kinds of people you'd like to be surrounded by; how much privacy you need, and how much interaction; what kinds of help you'd like; what kinds of responses you'd want to your ideas.

In your ideal environment, you might need to be challenged or maybe just really listened to or respected. You might want to be a teacher with the opportunity to inspire your students; or you might like to be a learner, surrounded by people who could teach you all kinds of fascinating things. You might want to be in charge of a large operation staffed by totally cooperative, efficient, loyal people who are keen to do whatever you tell them to. Or you might prefer to be a member of an egalitarian group effort. It's entirely up to you.

Letting the environment do the work for you means not changing yourself in this script. Above all, don't try to improve yourself in this scenario. Improve the world, so that your characteristics stop being problems. If you hate doing household chores, don't imagine yourself being more self-disciplined or patient. Imagine eight little monkeys or Honda Asimov robots following you around cleaning up after you! Feel free to be as whimsical or even silly—this is your script, so everything is allowed.

If you're a procrastinator (like me sometimes), or tend to panic in the face of deadlines, or if you are impatient and don't like it when things around you stay the same, don't think of these traits as character weaknesses that need changing. Think of them as design problems—challenges to your ingenuity as a world-maker. Create an environment that fits and supports you as you are, so that you are comfortable, secure and free to turn in your best performance.

After you've imagined your ideal environment, do one more thing: list a few adjectives telling what positive qualities in you—intellectual, emotional, creative—would emerge if you were in that environment. ("loving", "assertive", "playful", "productive", "serene", "independent", etc.)

Picture yourself operating at the peak of your powers. If you find yourself asking "who am I to want the best life?" simply acknowledge that this is just your self-talk, which is irrepressible. Ignore your self-talk and allow your imagination free rein as you continue to script your ideal environment.

Try it yourself: Life Scripting 2 – describing your perfect day

Armed with the information you've gathered from the "20 things I enjoy doing exercise" and "Life Scripting 1" above, now think about how you would spend your time and who you would spend it with. What sorts of things would you be doing?

Just really quickly, before you launch into describing your perfect day, remember that this technique is more than simple wishing or day dreaming. You are about to script, to write out, your perfect day. So you must write everything in the first person, present tense. Also describe events visually and sequentially as they take place during your perfect day. This same principle applies for the Goal Listing technique I teach in the following chapter. In describing your perfect day, you're actually seeing everything that's happening around you; you're really feeling and experiencing every sensation that you would if this were happening for real. In your perfect day, time passes the same way as it does in real life, but faster.

For example: "This is awesome! I'm sitting here with "X" million dollars. Let's see. What shall I do first?....Ok, I'm in a mansion on a hill above the sea. My airplane is in a little hangar behind the house. I can see my sailboat rocking down at the dock. It's a cool, sunny morning, and the whole day stretches ahead of me...."

With pen in hand and as much paper as you need, take a leisurely walk through a day that would be perfect if it represented your ideal days—not a vacation day, not a compromise day, but the very substance of your life as you'd love it to be. Live through that day in the present tense and in detail, from getting up in the morning to going to sleep at night. What's the first thing you do when you wake up? What do you have for breakfast? Do you make it yourself—or is it brought to you in bed, with the morning paper? Do you take a long, hot bath? a bracing cold shower? What kinds of clothes do you put on? How do you spend the morning? the afternoon? At each time of day, are you indoors or outdoors, quiet or active, alone or with people?

Technique Three: Life Scripting

Let's suppose you want to earn $100,000 a year in passive or investment income. Do you know what that really looks like for you? How much is that a month? What does the weekly pay check look like? What's your tax bill? What kind of house would you live in? What car(s) would you be driving? How would that change the interaction you have with those you love?

Or suppose your dream is to change careers, or to travel and live in another country. What would your average day be like? What would you be doing?

The more you can really see your abundance, the more likely you are to attract it. Write a movie script of your perfect day.

As you go through the hours of your perfect day, there are three helpful categories to keep in mind: what, where, and who.

- What are you doing—what kind of work, what kind of play? Imagine yourself at the full stretch of your capacities. If you'd like to sing or sail, and you don't know how, in this fantasy you do know how.

- Where—in what kind of place, space, situation? An inner-city apartment, a country farm, a fully-equipped workshop, an elegant hotel room, a houseboat?

- Who do you work, eat, laugh, talk, and sleep with?

You will undoubtedly want to write some of your favorite real people in your fantasy; you might also want to include some types of people you'd like to be surrounded by—writers, musicians, children, people your own age, people of all different ages, athletes, financiers, country people, celebrities.

Just as you did with your ideal environment, turn your imagination loose. Don't put down what you think is possible—

put down the kind of day you'd like to live if you had absolute freedom, unlimited means, and all the powers and skills you've ever wished for.

Stuff that would be minutiae in a real Hollywood script is very important to you. So, don't hold back on any details. You want a compelling and thorough journaling of your perfect day—the day you want to manifest. You want to see it, hear it, taste it, smell it, touch it and feel it. It is only when you experience abundance and accomplishment in your mind and heart first, that you manifest it on the physical plain.

Your script will center you, calm you, and reinforce the positive programming in your subconscious mind. This is a very powerful tool for accepting your abundance.

Life Scripting Debrief

By simply writing and describing your ideal environment and day, you've just taken the first – and most important – step toward designing, creating, and realizing your perfect life. Using the other WriteTech techniques, you will learn how to write down your vision for your life, create a map showing you the way to that vision, and identify goals that will be in harmony with that vision. You will also learn amazing writing techniques—tapping into the Superconscious Mind, capturing valuable ideas, discernment and many others—that you can use along the journey toward your life vision, your perfect life.

Now let's analyze the information you've gained from both Life Scripting lessons. This analysis will yield rich clues that will guide you in the process of Goal Listing, which comes in the following chapter. So, let's go ahead and do it.

Technique Three: Life Scripting

Analyzing your ideal environment

Everything ever created was first designed. And everything that was ever designed was first thought of, as an idea in someone's mind. If you want to eventually create your ideal environment and actually be in it one day, then you must first design it. That is what you just did in the Life Scripting I technique.

What did you learn about yourself and the things you need around you so that you could perform at your very best all the time? Even if you included some playful, fantastic elements in there, or inserted extras, like activities you've never done before but would love to do or objects that you've never ever owned but would love to own, all this is giving you clues of what you truly need if you are to function at your best.

The optimum environment for you will be one that provides real equivalents for all the major, indispensable features of your fantasy (read on and I'll help guide you to distinguish between what are major, indispensable elements from optional ones and pure extras). You have a right to this environment and the WriteTech techniques taught in this book will help you create that environment.

Certainly, the actual process of creating your optimum environment will involve more than simply shutting your eyes and daydreaming. It's going to involve you taking the individual elements of your ideal environment and turning them into concrete goals that you can pursue and achieve. It will require you to write down a vision of your ideal life and specifying the components of each individual area of your life. And once this is all written down, it's going to entail you being ready to take inspired action on ideas and plans as they come to you along the way. But most challenging of all, this process will necessitate dealing with stubborn, resistant substances like time and money, habit and fear—and the most stubborn of all, other people.

Don't let this discourage you though. Believe it or not, all these inner and outer obstacles can be overcome. That's purely a matter of strategy, planning and execution. But before strategy, planning and execution come fantasy, dreaming, scripting.

Without a dream, how do you know where you want to go? And until you do, how can you sit down and plan how to get there? Before you can go somewhere, you first have to imagine exactly "where" that somewhere is.

Analyzing your perfect day

The Life Scripting 2 exercise invited you to embellish your ideal day with everything and everyone you could think of that would make that day just perfect. But if you dig a little deeper, you'll see that some of the elements you included may be more important or indispensable to you than the others. Let's identify what they are and then later I'll show you how to work with them.

First let's separate the totally indispensable elements of your perfect day, from the desirable but optional ones, and then from the purely extras.

- Question 1: in each of the three categories—what, where and who—which elements of your ideal day are absolutely indispensable? That is, which elements are absolutely required for you to be happy, and without which you would never be satisfied?
- Question 2: which elements are desirable but optional?
- Question 3: which elements are purely extras—that is, they would be good to have around, but if they weren't there, you wouldn't long for them and you could still be happy?

Let's say after scripting your ideal day, you've identified the separate elements that make up that day. On your journal or computer document, you might write a table like the example below:

Indispensable

What (activities)   Writing

    Physical exercise

    Pets

Where (places)   A private study with a big desk

    A spacious living area

Who (people)   My husband or wife

Optional but desirable

What (activities)   Learn to play guitar

Where (places)   Live in the country near a culturally-lively town

    A spacious living area

Who (people)   Lots of friends near and far

Purely extras

What (activities)   The horse

    The printing press

Where (places)   My own country house

Separating the elements of your ideal day into indispensable, desirable and extra doesn't mean you only get to have some but not all of them! Don't think that categorizing the elements this way is compromising between what you can and can't have. It is not compromising. I completely believe that you should have every single element of your perfect day, yes, even the extras, the stuff that you'd be thrilled to have but will not long for if you didn't.

What you've just done here is prioritize your elements—we're separating the elements you cannot live without and are totally required for you to be happy. These are the things that you should pour your full energies into getting first; you should also get them as quickly as possible so you will have lots of energy, passion and enthusiasm to purse the other elements.

Not every fantasy day can be broken down this neatly. However your fantasy breaks down, our next task is to measure the distance between your life as you now live it and the minimum ideal day that would make you happy.

- Question 4: What happens when you walk through an adjusted dream day with only the indispensable elements in it?

Once you've distilled your perfect day down to its indispensable elements, there are three more important questions to ask about it.

- Question 5: Do you already have any of those indispensable elements?

Very few of us are totally discontented with the status quo. Some of our wishes and choices have managed to find their way into reality. This question shows you what's already going right with your life. In *Chapter 10 Discernment of the Spirits*, I write about consolations (people, things and conditions that bring us peace,

Technique Three: Life Scripting

contentment, joy and satisfaction) and desolations (things that bring us the opposite). If you pause and reflect, you will see that you might already have many sources of consolation in your life. Your consolations will be your starting point. They will be your anchors and sources of energy as you start pursuing the desirable but optional, and later the purely extra elements, of your perfect day.

- Question 6: What elements of the adjusted perfect day are glaringly missing from your life right now? Use the three categories—what, where, who—to help you pinpoint what's missing.

Now you've got fantasy and reality matched up, you can compare them. You may have learned that your present life isn't as far off the mark as you thought it was; or you may have confirmed that you really are years away from your destination. Either way, now you know exactly what's missing and what you've got to work with. Fantasy and reality are now in focus as well as stark contrast. We will now look at the gap between them. For the first time in this chapter, I'll now ask you to "be realistic".

- Question 7: What stands between you and having your adjusted perfect day tomorrow? That is, what would it take to get all the missing elements? What problems or obstacles are presently stopping you from getting them? What are the barriers standing between you and your adjusted perfect day—the minimum "what", "where" and "who" that would make you happy?

Get Goal-ing!

I couldn't resist the pun sorry! I just think it sets up the next chapter on Goal Setting nicely.

Ok, so now that you know how you want your perfect day to go and exactly what kind of environment you want to function in, it's time to start molding that fantasy day into something you can grasp and start going after. It's time to write down some goals.

Technique Four: GoalSeek

A powerful goal setting paradigm

Have you ever set a goal for yourself, something that you truly wanted to achieve, but didn't? Do you know someone or have you ever heard of someone who seems to have an uncanny ability to achieve whatever goals they've set? Have you ever wondered how they can do this?

The reason I believe is because the majority of goals are easily stirred and blown over by winds of adversity and trial, and because they are not anchored on something immovable and unshakable within a person. I believe any goal, if firmly anchored in this way, will be achieved.

Boundaries, hindrances, and passages

One of the definitions of 'goal' is "an observable and measurable end result having one or more objectives to be achieved within a more or less fixed timeframe". Along similar lines are the definitions given by Oxford Dictionary: "the object of a person's ambition or effort; an aim or desired result" and even "the destination of a journey".

But 'goal' was not always defined in these above figurative senses. The etymology of "goal" suggests that roots of this word can be traced as far back as the 1530s, when it meant "end point of a race". According to the Online Etymology Dictionary, the word 'gol' appeared once in a 14th century poem, with the sense of being a "boundary" or "limit". The modern word 'goal' could also have originated from the Old English "gal", which means "obstacle" or "barrier", which is implied by "gælan", meaning "to hinder". According to the same dictionary, the word as defined would make it a variant or figurative use of the Middle English word "gale", that is, "a way" or "course". This could also be compared with the Old Norse "geil", which means "a narrow passage". Both the sports sense of "goal" (as a place where the ball is put to score) and figurative sense (as an "object of effort") appear to have originated from the 1540s.

A reading of the etymology of the word 'goal' is revealing; surprisingly, it also holds clues as to the true nature of goals, why they are so important in our lives, and why they are often difficult to achieve. A goal can be understood as the "end point of a race", which signifies it's something that we reach after a period of pursuit; it is an end in itself.

But understood as a "limit", a goal signifies something that represents the outer barrier of what we can achieve in a particular area of life. Limits or barriers, however, are never static; once they are breached, there is always a new limit or barrier to reach and break. Take for instance the human goal of running a mile in less than 4 minutes. This was thought impossible until British middle-distance runner Roger Bannister did it on May 6, 1954. Less than a year after he did it, another person ran the sub-4 minute mile. Then more people did it. Now it's no longer even considered unusual and runners are trying to achieve increasingly faster speeds.

As a "hindrance", a goal is something that we must pass or overcome before we can move on to the next, higher level. But rather than being a stage that we reach or something that must be overcome, perhaps it is better to think about a goal in the sense of the Middle English "gale", which is a "way" or, even the Old Norse "geil", which is a "narrow passage". Our goal may be achieved in the process of our pursuit of it; the point of achieving the goal lies not in accomplishing an objective or a target, but in the inner transformation that takes place on the journey toward the goal.

In the next two sections, we will go through the process of seeking goals and then listing down these goals in a way that will ensure you achieve them faster than you ever thought possible.

GoalSeeking

Before I started giving WriteTech seminars, I had assumed that everyone had goals and had them written down on paper or digitally somewhere. But through my seminars, I've realized that this is not the case. I was surprised to find out of every five people I asked, four didn't have a written list of concrete goals they wanted to achieve or had not written their goals down on paper.

So, I'm assuming that you already know or have your goals and listed them down. But if not, I've written this section to help you come up with your list of goals. If you already have specific and concrete goals and written them down, then this section is optional; but I encourage you to read it anyway – I'm certain it will help you refine, and give you new insights on the goals you already have.

The late Barbara Sher, who I mentioned in the previous chapter, describes a goal as a "basic unit of life design". I think this an accurate way of defining what a goal is. Think about your life now, where you are, which degree you completed, which college or university you attended, the type of job you're doing or business you're running, where you live, the kinds of relationships you're enjoying, and the activities you're engaging in. Chances are, you didn't end up with any of these things or people just because you chanced upon them or they came randomly or by accident. At one point, you thought that you'd like to go to that particular university and study that degree; you thought it would be good to have this kind of job or that kind of business; you imagined how nice it would be to have a relationship with this kind of person or to live in this kind of house or environment. If you've thought about any of these things at any point in your life, then you've already set goals. And if you've accomplished many of your goals, then their sum total is now your present life experience.

Some people though find themselves aimlessly drifting from one relationship or job to the next; others are unable to stay in any single place, even though they really want to build their life in one place. It's perfectly all right if your number one goal in life is to have freedom to move around, experience variety in everything and never be tied down. But if the reason you're drifting from one relationship, job or place to the next is because you don't have a goal of where you really want to be, what you really want to do, and who you really want to do it with, then you need to set some goals for yourself.

Still other people are serial goal-setters, but not serial goal-achievers. They set one resolution or goal after another, start on some of them, run out of steam at some point, abandon a goal, move on to the next one, and repeat the whole process all over again. This is fine if this comes as a natural process of evolution of your goals. As I stress throughout this chapter, our goals are not meant to be written in stone; they are ever evolving.

It's also great if the reason you drop goals is because you've already achieved them or something greater, and have now set even loftier goals. It's also fine if you dropped a goal midway because you realized that this goal was too small for you or it no longer resonates with where you are in your life. It's different though if you set one goal after another but never end up achieving any of them. Achieving a goal generates a tremendous feeling of pride, confidence and accomplishment and galvanizes our energies to go after bigger goals. But dropping a goal, something that we truly want, midway creates the opposite effect—it causes us to lose self-confidence, can make us feel defeated and deflated, and discourages us from pursuing further goals.

If a goal is a basic unit of life design, then you can easily design your dream life by listing down all the individual goals that will collectively comprise your dream life. But it's very difficult, if not impossible, to list down every possible unit of our dream life; besides, you can't predict how your tastes and preferences will change in the future, so it's not practical to be so specific in some goals at this stage when you're still trying to identify what your goals are.

If you want to make your dream life real, you must start by choosing the one most important and indispensable unit of that life and commit to achieving that one. In his book *The Success Principles*, American author and trainer Jack Canfield calls this the Breakthrough Goal. I've had the pleasure of being a student of Jack's coaching program; it has helped me define and achieve several breakthrough goals. But instead of a breakthrough goal, I will call this your *overriding goal* – the one goal that overrides all others and that you must accomplish before all other goals can be accomplished; it's the one goal that must be in your dream life for it to be complete.

A true overriding goal meets several important criteria:

Criterion 1: a goal is specific and concrete

Whether you've achieved a goal or not is a question of fact. When you've set a goal, you will know that you've achieved it if you can see it, touch it, and show it to others. If your goal is to "one day run a business or be a business owner", that's still a dream. An actual goal will be: "to open my own restaurant or launch my online retail store in six months". There's nothing ambiguous about it. In six months, you will either have opened that restaurant or launched that online store or not; that's how you know you've achieved that goal.

Criterion 2: a goal is time-stamped

Your overriding goal has to be a specific and concrete event, thing or experience. You also need to set a date or a period when that goal will be achieved so that you'll know for certain when you've achieved it. By choosing a date, you're also setting yourself up to succeed and meet it in advance. Choosing a date is the start of all effective project planning. It is the number one cure for procrastination and frustration. By putting a date, you can set separate tasks that you need to achieve to get the goal by your due date. Each time you tick off a task, then you have a sense of accomplishment and feel good because you've moved a step closer to your goal.

It's not a requirement that you time-stamp a specific date to your goal. You can put a period or a season. Australian public speaker, trainer and founder of Authentic Education, Ben Harvey, said that the timing of goals can be cyclical; he explains that while men work better when they link goals to specific dates (for example by April 1 of some future year), women achieve goals better when they are linked to cycles (for example, "by the end of summer"). This makes sense in my experience. But it's by no means a hard and fast rule. See what works for you.

But you must time-stamp your goal; when you do, time suddenly becomes your ally, as well as an element that you can work with. Since you've set a date to your goal, you wouldn't want to miss that deadline.

Criterion 3: a goal needs no justification

A goal must be 100% true to who you are. If you say you want to produce your own movie that you've written, launch your own quirky clothing brand, author a best-selling weight loss book, or achieve financial independence in 36 months (all goals set by my seminar students), you're not kidding. What you desire is what you want. You don't need to justify or explain the reasons to anyone but yourself, and you certainly shouldn't apologize or explain to anyone why you want it.

And because your goal is true to you, it is extremely personal. Only you can decide when you've achieved it and what it means to you. The only person who has to be happy when the goal is achieved is you.

How do you know if you truly want that goal? Well, it's like the Oracle said to Neo in the movie *The Matrix:* "You know because you feel it in your bones". But what if you want to test the goal? You can try an exercise called "sacred visualizations", which I explain in *Chapter 10 Discernment of the Spirits.* For example, your goal, which you've written down on paper, is to "be the CEO of my own multinational company". Now you want to check whether this is a real overriding goal that will stand the test of time or merely a capricious passing whim. Then you have to test it by visualizing it, and living it in detail. Imagine things in the first person, you're doing things in the present time, and going through a typical day sequentially, just as you would if you really are the CEO of your own multinational company. This is the litmus test for any goal: imagining it's already yours and checking how you feel. If you still feel ecstatic after imagining your day as CEO in great detail, then go for it. That's an overriding goal. But if you're not feeling as pumped because you're thinking it will take you away from your family, then change the goal! You might realize that what you wanted all along is the freedom of owning and running a successful business, but not necessarily a multinational company.

Yes, you must have what you want, no explanations required. But you must actually like that goal and not merely think that it would be nice to have it. This makes going after it so much easier and fun.

Criterion 4: a goal is meant to stretch you

Remember that one of the early roots of the word 'goal' is 'gol', which means a boundary or limit. By its very nature, a goal is meant to stretch you and test your limits, and extend you beyond your comfort zone. I'm not dismissing small goals; certainly, any worthwhile goal that we set for ourselves, whether small or big, deserves our sincere effort and commitment.

But I'm referring to goals that excite and terrify you at the same time; goals that send your pulse racing, make your heart skip several beats, fill your stomach with a thousand butterflies…you get the point. Goals that make you want to jump out of bed every morning and look with anticipation toward their achievement. A goal which, when you think of accomplishing it, fills you with passion. A goal the very thought of which fills you with a deep sense of peace, because it resonates with something deep in the core of you. A goal that challenges and tests you, that might even make you doubt your own abilities, but which you know deep inside, is achievable, somehow, someway.

A mentor once told me that with truly grand goals, if you start off having an idea of how to achieve them, then they are not grand enough. These goals are never easy to achieve; getting them will require lots of commitment, persistence, hard work, creative thinking, external help and, sometimes, even a shovelful of luck. In a word, the kind of goal I'm talking about is a *grand goal*. And what's grand is relative to the person setting them; setting a goal of making a million dollars this financial year may be small to someone who has done it many times before, but it will be a mountain for anyone who has never even earned more than a hundred thousand dollars a year.

Also, if you find that you're achieving every single big goal you've set for yourself in the last five years, it could be that you're an amazing specimen of a human being, in which case, you should go for even bigger goals. Or it could be because the size of your goals is not grand enough, and that you're not being stretched enough. Conversely, when you're finding that you're not achieving any goal at all, it could either be a commitment or self-discipline issue or you're setting goals that are too big for you, at least given your present situation and resources. Only you can decide which goals are grand enough and truly worthy of your one hundred percent commitment and effort to pursue.

Criterion 5: a goal is a touchstone

According to Dictionary.com, a touchstone is "a black siliceous stone formerly used to test the purity of gold and silver by the color of the streak produced on it by rubbing it with either metal."

You use a touchstone by getting a stone of known purity, for example gold or silver, then rubbing that on your touchstone, and observing the color or brightness of the streak that it leaves on the stone. And when you want to compare another stone with the pure one you have, you do the same thing and compare the quality of the streak it leaves, whether it's the same or duller than the original streak. In the hands of an expert, a touchstone can reveal whether a precious stone is pure or not.

A goal acts in much the same way; it can act as a touchstone to what you value most or hold dearest in your heart. I believe that it's the goals that are tied to the things that you value or consider most precious in your life that stick; these are the ones that you must achieve come hell or high water, the ones that will not stay quiet or give you peace until you go after them and achieve them.

In my WriteTech seminars and workshops, when my participants and I do this GoalSeek exercise, we go through a game called "SWSWSW…Next!" You can try it too: name a goal that you want to get right now, for example, to be a movie or TV star. Then ask, "so why do I want this goal?" After each response, again ask "so why do I want this?" Keep asking until you reach the emotional core of your goal. That's your touchstone. In the movie or TV star goal for example, after playing the "SWSWSW…Next!" game, you might dig deeper and realize that the reason you want this is to receive acclaim, honor and recognition for your acting. But ultimately, you arrive at the core goal of feeling fantastic and excited when people tell you you're a great actor.

Tony Robbins in his audio program *Unlimited Power II: The Driving Force* makes a great point about this: ultimately, the core of any goal is to achieve an emotional state. You don't really want to be a famous actor as an ultimate end in itself; what if you find that one day you are already a famous actor. Is it all right if for the next five years you could keep being famous, but no one ever watched you at work in that time? No, because that wouldn't be good at all; for you the pleasure of being famous lies in feeling good because people praise you for how good you are or because they tell you how much they enjoy watching you act. This feeling, this state is your touchstone goal. This is what's most important to you about that goal; this is the value behind that goal. That's the goal you go after first, because this is the goal that will give you what you most desire right now. So, you see, you don't have to wait until you get your goal of becoming a famous actor to enjoy the touchstone of that goal.

You can experience that touchstone goal right now by acting in your local theater or starting your own YouTube channel and building a base of admiring fans. Think of these as preparation, as the dress rehearsal for the grand performance that will one day come. By doing these preparatory acts, you generate the state that the grand goal will create (excitement, pride, passion, etc.), not in the future, but right now.

If you prioritize living your touchstone goal every day, then it would make the way to reaching your big goal of becoming a famous actor more fun. Imagine the countless moments of pleasure you'll experience every time you live your touchstone goal of feeling good when someone praises your acting. Even if ultimately, you don't even end up being a Hollywood A-lister, you wouldn't really care because you've been basking in the adoration and praise of your admirers for years—and that's what you truly wanted anyway.

The touchstone goal is something reliable that you can always fall back on when things get difficult on the way to your grand goal. If trials and adversity come along the way, you will not feel discouraged, because all the while, you've been enjoying the experience of living your touchstone goal. All along, living your touchstone goal has been making you happy. And ultimately, isn't being happy what we all truly want to be? When you get to the essence of a grand goal, and endeavor to live that essence every day, then any grand goal, even if it looks impossible, becomes possible.

Try the technique yourself: GoalSeek

Now let's choose some goals that are truly worthy of you.

Touchstone method:

Step 1: Take any goal you want, the bigger the better. Write down that goal in your journal.

Step 2: Subject it to the "SWSWSW…Next!" process: keep asking why you want this goal and write down your answers; keep asking and writing until you reach the touchstone goal. This goal becomes your first target: a modest goal that brings you closer to your grand goal and at the same time is a nice win by itself.

Step 3: On a fresh page, write down the touchstone goal and underline it. Then list down every way you can think of that could possibly bring you that touchstone.

Step 4: Rank each way you come up with in terms of what's most doable right now. You can even build a table and beside each action, you list down in bullet points:

- what's useful about this action
- any challenges to achieve this
- what this action tells me about myself
- am I willing to do this action now, and
- any other notes and suggestions

Then you take things from there. Sooner or later, you will come up with a list of sub-goals that you can take action on right now; by consistently taking action on, and achieving these sub-goals, you start shaping that seemingly grand or impossible goal into an eminently possible one.

Bite-sizing method:

This is the method for you if at first your goal is so broad, you don't know where to start. Recall the 'LifeScripting' techniques we did in Chapter Three, where you described and wrote down your perfect day or even the Vision for your life you will write in *Chapter 8 Vision Mapping*. Well, what if that's your grand goal – to one day live that perfect day in every single detail or be in a position to always live perfect days like that every day? Or what if your ultimate goal is to achieve that life vision? That's all right. You break down your perfect day into small chunks. No doubt you've heard that the only way to eat an entire elephant is one bite at a time.

Step 1: Go through the description that you wrote of your ideal day.

Step 2: Among the elements of that ideal day, which ones are indispensable, the highest-priority items that are absent from your life at this moment? Write those elements down. These become your first targets.

Step 3: Among these elements you listed, which one can you get in the cheapest, easiest and fastest way possible? This becomes square one, your starting point. This is the first chunk of the elephant that you'll eat.

The objective is to start you on your grand goal without delay. If you take this first step, if you take that first bite, you'll be led toward the next element of your grand goal, that perfect day or ideal life vision, and the next and the next. Soon, you'll gain momentum and draw toward you the people, resources and things you need to help move you further along the path to your grand goal.

Try it yourself: GoalList

Successful people credit writing down their goals as the single most important thing they did to be able to achieve those goals. Brian Tracy in his book *Goals!* even goes so far as saying that a goal that is not written is not a goal at all. "Everyone who succeeds greatly works from clear, written, specific detailed goals and plans, reviewed regularly, sometimes every day," Tracy explains.

As I described in *Chapter Two Writing to the 100th Power*, I strongly recommend that you write your goals every day, if possible for a hundred days or even longer until you achieve them. This act embeds your goals into your subconscious mind, and unknown to you, also impresses them upon the Superconscious Mind. I'll talk more about the Superconscious Mind in Chapter 6. Once this happens, your goals will take on a life of their own and become supercharged.

Step 1: Compose your own list of goals. You can do this anywhere, anytime. But preferably choose a quiet place where you won't be disturbed. Use the 5 criteria listed above for each goal.

Step 2: Write fast. Do not linger over the page. If you find yourself dismissing a goal as too grand or impractical, write it down anyway and underline or put an asterisk next to it. That may be a goal worth committing to.

Step 3: Time-stamp each goal. Set a deadline for the achievement of each goal and write down that goal in the present tense as if it has already been achieved, and inject verbs or active descriptors of what you're feeling, like this:

> "It is the (state the specific date or cycle). I feel (state verb or descriptor of what you're feeling) as I now am/have (state the specific goal—the experience or thing—you've set)."

A deadline is a "guesstimate" of when you think that goal will be achieved. It's like trying to shoot an arrow at the bull's eye. Sometimes you might hit it and sometimes you might go wide.

Technique Four: GoalSeek

You might find that you achieve several of your goals before your deadline, and some, after it. That's ok. The deadline is not meant to chain you to anything; no date or, for that matter, no goal is written in stone or in blood. But if you're going to achieve your goal, you must set a due date.

Step 4: After listing each goal, write down at least one definite and concrete action that you can take now toward that goal. Action carries great power that can propel you faster toward your goal. And as you follow the method I strongly recommended and write your goals every day, then every day too you'll be doing something concrete and before you know it, it is your goal that seems to be moving closer and closer to you.

One final reminder: don't overcomplicate this technique. Just write. Reach as deep into your core as possible. Do not be afraid of wanting too much. Write down even those ambitions which have no practical means of accomplishment. Keep on writing. Write from your heart and make the list as long as you like. Give yourself permission to dream, to be totally unrealistic. List whatever grandiose schemes you can come up with – if money were no object and time were not a factor. I'll write it again: in truth, money is no object, and time is not a factor. What you want can be achieved; there is a way—if you want it badly enough.

Technique Five: Gratitude Listing

Create your own miracle in 40 days

This chapter appears right after the chapter on Goal Listing, I did this deliberately. The reason for this is that the technique you will learn here will greatly amplify the power of the unique goal setting technique you learned in the previous chapter.

Stripping gratitude to the core

Melody Beattie, in her book *Make Miracles in 40 days* describes in detail the transformative power of writing about what you're grateful for even when it looks like your life is going down the drain. The idea of being grateful for the good things we receive, of feeling "blessed" when something favorable happens in our lives, has been promoted by many authors as well as the general media in the last decade; it has gained such traction and heavy publicity that we hear celebrities giving thanks to God when they receive a great honor like an award or a prize. It has become fashionable, even cool to publicly express gratitude when everything in your life is going well.

The mainstream media has preached how having an "attitude of gratitude" is the key to getting more material blessings, so much so that this expression has now become cliché. Being thankful has been so linked with getting material "stuff" back that it now risks being seen as shallow. It seems that if you want to get more money in a bank account, or a new car or boat or a bigger home, then being thankful is the veritable ATM card that will deliver these things to you.

In truth, though, practicing gratitude and being grateful have nothing to do with wanting something in return or getting something back. Being thankful is not something we do because we are expecting something in exchange; it is something that we must do because it is a law of the universe. There is a universal law of gratitude, which says that we should be grateful in every circumstance. Universal law mandates that we should be thankful, no matter what is happening to us, whether good or bad, and regardless of how we feel. And because it is law, consequences will flow whether it is obeyed or not.

The law of gratitude and thankfulness is timeless; it pervades virtually all human faiths and belief systems. The Christian bible says: "Rejoice always, pray continually, give thanks in all circumstances; for this is God's will for you in Christ Jesus." (1 Thessalonians 5:18). Biblical gratitude includes giving thanks always to God for all things (Ephesians 5:20). In the Muslim Quran, the first chapter starts with the word 'Alhamdulillah', which signifies gratitude in daily life. God also says in the Quran that "if you are thankful I will add more favors unto you." Buddhism teaches us to be grateful, without qualification or condition, and that gratitude is necessary for integrity. Hinduism names gratitude and appreciation as the two powers. One Hindu expression says: "Some people complain because God put thorns on roses. Others praise Him for putting roses among thorns". Even New Age gratitude holds that we can change reality by holding and cultivating a deep sense of gratitude, and that gratitude is the connecting link between us and the universe, infinite intelligence or infinite consciousness.

The critical thing about what these various faiths teach about gratitude is that it must be practiced constantly and for everything that happens in life. They teach that we should give thanks not only in times of good fortune but even in times of difficulties as well; we must be thankful in all things, not just for the good things, but for the seemingly bad and ugly things that happen as well.

I know some of you might be thinking, "you mean I should be thankful that I got laid off from my job or that my father or mother or child died or that I have cancer?" The technique I will teach in this chapter essentially involves writing about everything that we are grateful for. But it is true that there really are circumstances and situations when being thankful is inappropriate. The technique that I will share in this chapter includes a way to refocus what we're grateful or thankful for in in these situations.

Testing the law of gratitude

In *Chapter 2 Writing to the 100th Power*, I described a technique to achieve a specific outcome, which I used after I was fired from a job as a lawyer in 2015. That writing technique saved me and carried me through a period of uncertainty. That wasn't the only writing technique that I used though; the technique I will share in this chapter also helped me tremendously by encouraging me to focus on what was positive about my situation, and reminding me that there were so many good things already present in my life at the time I was fired. The technique also allowed me to set my sights on the silver lining on a dark horizon at the time. It forced me to keep a record of how good things increasingly came my way when I started keeping track of and listing what I was grateful for on a daily basis. This record is something that I can always refer back to as a reminder that I survived a challenging and uncertain period in my life and that I can thrive if something similar were to ever happen to me again.

A few days after I was fired, I wrote in my journal:

"Last Wednesday, I was unceremoniously fired from a job for the first time in my life. Looking back, due to the combination of factors that led to it, I'm not sure I could have prevented it. Maybe I would have delayed it if I knew then what I know now. But I feel it would've happened eventually anyway.

Since Friday, I've been trying to keep active – applying for teaching jobs, contacting my old professors, setting up meetings – anything to keep myself from thinking I was out of a job with no real prospects of getting another high paying job soon. Antonella and I are planning to go through the egg donor process in December in Greece – a $12,000 to $15,000 exercise. We wanted to save for a house deposit. My family was going to come here in September. I was going to visit them next month, to see them after 6 long years. Then I got fired from my job.

Yes, God, I do need a miracle, and I do need it in about 40 days. Before I start this process, I want to say thank you God for how you'll guide me to where I should go next, and for providing me with everything I'll need. Thank you for providing for everything Antonella will need too."

Technique Five: Gratitude Listing

It wasn't easy, at the moment I wrote this, to be thankful about anything. I felt a whole slew of feelings that were the diametric opposites of gratitude and thankfulness. I felt disappointment at having achieved a goal of landing a job in a Sydney law firm only to lose it in five months; bitterness at that law firm for making me undergo a humiliating experience; resentment toward the man who hired me, for unfairly criticizing my work and belittling my skills as a lawyer. And throw in a cocktail of other negative emotions in the mix – anger, revenge, doubt, despair, confusion, worry, anxiety; if it was something negative, I probably felt it too in the days following my job termination.

I was scared, confused and didn't know what to do next. I knew I needed guidance but I didn't have anyone to ask. I had taken a bank loan of $40,000 a few weeks before I lost my job, because even as early as then, I was already anticipating that I would not last in my job. Now I had no job, no income and had no visible means of paying what I owed. Yes, it was hard to be thankful for anything at that point. But it was what the technique required me to do—to practice gratitude for everything, including the things I didn't like and hated. This was at the heart of this miracle creation technique: I wasn't supposed to just write out my gratitude for the good things; that was easy. Instead, I also had to write out that I was thankful *especially* for those things that I wasn't feeling particularly thankful for.

On the first day of the 40-day process, I wrote:

Today I am grateful that –

1. I no longer have a job (it was hard to write this, believe me!).

2. I have been freed from a job that I despised (this was a bit easier to write).

3. I am confused about what to do next.

4. I don't know what to do next, where to go, which job or field to enter.

5. There are 3 options emerging for me – joining another firm, teaching or working for myself.

6. The option to work for myself for the first time in my life excites and scares me at the same time.

7. That I feel like after 10 years in Australia, I haven't made any progress – I don't have a job, no savings, have not yet built anything.

8. I have deep, deep desires and big, big dreams and ambitions and goals for my life.

9. I am healthy in mind and body, I am alive.

10. I have a woman who loves and supports me.

Maybe you can clearly grasp that I didn't feel grateful at all for majority of the things in my first list. The technique sounded counter-intuitive, crazy even. But I had nothing to lose. Within me I had the unshakable sense that despite what logic and reason were shouting in my ear, my spirit told me that I must stop worrying and feeling sorry for myself, that I must stop resisting, and that I must instead be thankful for being exactly where I was and what I had in my life until that point.

My Aikido training helped me as well. All those years of training leading up to my blackbelt were finally going to pay off when I needed it to. Aikido preached non-resistance to opposing forces as the first step to gaining control of them. Once controlled, the opposing force can be channeled and redirected back to the

Technique Five: Gratitude Listing

source. The words of many of my teachers now came back to me, reminding me of the single most important life lesson of Aikido: "relax completely; keep your center; extend your energy forward." I was taught that resistance was the fastest way to block one's Ki (or life force, the positive energy of the universe) from flowing to me. This was by no means a unique teaching to Aikido. Countless belief systems have all taught that resistance is the most potent way to unplug from the universe, God, Allah, Infinite Intelligence, or the Creator. Resistance blocks our good from coming to us, destroys our power and prevents us from moving forward.

I realized then that I was feeling so miserable in my situation because I was resisting everything that was happening, because I objected to the state of things as they presently were. I wasn't supposed to be fired, was supposed to be making more money, and was supposed to have already built a good life for myself after a decade in Australia! All this resistance was building up in me and it eventually became a physical, not just an emotional, weight I had to carry. Resisting started becoming painful; but on the other hand, relaxing about everything to the point of surrendering to circumstances as they were, actually felt good.

So, I threw myself utterly and completely to the 40-day miracle technique. I figured I had nothing to lose. As required by the technique, I should say I was grateful for all things, exactly as they were. I'd stick out the 40 days, and see how things went. That first day, the miracle that I asked for was for my aimlessness, confusion, searching and wandering to be replaced with a crystal-clear vision, diamond-hard purpose, absolute clarity, and total certainty that I knew my true purpose in life. But that wasn't all that I asked for:

> *I want to pursue my purpose steadfastly and relentlessly, letting it guide my work, career and calling, and allowing it to direct every other area of my life. And more than that – I desire to pursue my calling with passion and zeal and*

never grow weary because it is founded on my true purpose in life. I ask God to tell me, in unequivocal words, what my life purpose is, the one thing that he put me on this earth to do, my life calling.

Every night after that first day, I wrote down my list of things I was grateful for. C.S. Lewis once wrote:

I pray because I can't help myself. I pray because I'm helpless. I pray because the need flows out of me all the time, working and sleeping. It doesn't change God. It changes me.

This is exactly what I did. Every time I wrote, I prayed. Every time I listed things, persons and events that I was grateful for, I prayed. I couldn't help it. I was helpless. It was through my writing that I reached out to God for help.

I'm not going to lie and say that I felt grateful all the time during this 40-day exercise. There were many days, certainly on those days when absolutely nothing seemed to be happening, that it was a chore to write. But I forced myself to write what I was grateful for, even though many times, I felt like I was faking it or lying to myself. When it was hard to write that I was grateful for something, I instead wrote, "today, I give thanks for…" because that way, I wouldn't be lying. I merely wrote 'thank you' for things, people and events, because I remembered that 'in all things, give thanks'.

The 'ripple effect'

I heard a speech delivered by a friend and colleague of mine from my local Toastmasters club about how the things we do, even

Technique Five: Gratitude Listing

the seemingly small, inconsequential things, create ripples in the world. Throw a pebble into a pond and see it create ripples. Throw other pebbles right after the first one, and you create ripples too many to count; you cannot know with certainty how all these ripples will interact and affect each other. Our small acts, whether good or bad, are these pebbles, and their consequences are the ripples. Every little thing we do creates effects and has consequences.

For me, writing every night for 40 days and nights was a pebble that created ripples; every item on my list that I said I was thankful for was another ripple-creating pebble. I had been writing so many things that I was thankful or grateful for that it became impossible to trace exactly which of them created the ripples that would eventually bring about my miracle. Looking back now at that time, I can't tell you which ripples caused by other people's acts eventually came back to me, delivering the miracle I had asked for.

I can't remember how things developed; events took place so naturally and effortlessly that I didn't even notice that things were indeed happening for my good. Whatever I needed was provided; all that I required was given. Existing contacts introduced me to other people, who, in turn, opened doors for me, giving me the opportunities I needed. In many instances, I was urged, led, even inspired by what I am absolutely certain was an external guiding influence, to do a specific act, or call a specific person. In many cases, I was prompted to call someone I had not spoken to in years or even a complete stranger. Doing so led to even further good opportunities and opened other doors for me.

Unaided, I wouldn't have been able to remember every single good thing as it came to me; luckily, I had my writing, my lists on paper to remind me, indelible records that the miracle I had asked for started coming to me from day one.

By the 40th day, several significant things had already happened: I had found three teaching jobs, one of them at one of the most prestigious universities in Sydney; I was getting paid double, even triple what I used to earn at my former job, I had saved a 5-figure amount; and I had plenty of time to plan my next steps since all my jobs were part-time. But above all, the miracle that I had originally desired – to know my true life purpose – had now happened. When I first started this process, I was scared that I wouldn't survive, that I would sink. But now 40 days after, not only was I surviving, I was thriving, succeeding, and moving forward with my life!

In the early days of practicing the technique, I found myself faking gratitude often. But now my gratitude had become real. I had learned a truly priceless lesson: that I could create miracles from what I had, starting from where I was. I had witnessed first-hand the truth of a promise that my mother had taught her children to memorize from when we were very young: "that all things work for the good of those who believe". Indeed, for me, they had.

Try it yourself: 40-day miracle technique

I give credit to Melody Beattie's 40 day miracle creation method for its tremendous impact on my life. I have modified and tested it to fit my own needs and found it amazingly effective and powerful. Test it yourself and adopt it to your own situation and circumstances. I promise you won't be disappointed. There are seven steps:

Step 1: Commit to the process for at least 40 days.

Write down the starting and end dates on your journal, diary or calendar. Time is a crucial factor for a couple of techniques shown in this book: *Chapter 2 Writing to the 100th Power* requires continuous writing for 100 days; this chapter's technique needs at least 40 days. The reasons behind the day requirements are explained in the individual chapters.

Technique Five: Gratitude Listing

Whether you sense that things are progressing or nothing seems to be happening at all and the 40 days are up, I encourage you to continue. You can never expect when the breakthrough you are looking for will come; it could come before the 40th day or sometime after. Even if you keep writing well past the 40th day, you'll reap many benefits by using the technique I describe here. The best and most important benefit is that it will help you see all the good things in your life and be truly grateful for each and every one of them.

Step 2: Answer this question, "what do you want?"

I'm fairly certain that by now, you already recognize the amazing power of writing. Unleashing that power is a matter of involving all your senses, as well as your imagination, and even your inner voices as you write. The Bible records Jesus Christ as asking more than 173 questions, which can be reduced to 7 essential ones. There is one question that shows up in seven verses in the Bible and it is the one question Jesus asked more than any other:

"What do you want?"

A variation of this question is "what do you want me to do for you?" Regardless of your faith, whether you believe in a higher power, God or the Universe, or whether you simply believe in yourself, I believe asking these questions to yourself and answering them can, literally, transform your life. Jesus here is a symbol of the highest possibilities of ourselves, our highest potentialities asking us, "what do you want?", "what do you need?", "what are you looking for?"

If no one, not even yourself, has asked this question of you before, I urge you to ask it now and to really think about your answer. Be specific in what you ask for. Write your request down. Even if the answer is obvious ("I need a job!" or "I want to get well!"), write it down anyway. Often, you will find that the very act of writing down your request awakens your faith and signifies your belief that it will be granted. Whether the request is personal, and even selfish in nature, ask it. If there are several things you want, ask for those too. And if you don't know exactly what you want, only that you want things to get better, that's fine, ask for that. When you become clearer on what you want, you can refine your questions. And as with everything in this book, write it down, write it all down.

Step 3: Determine if you'll go through this process by yourself or with a partner.

Either way is equally effective and each one has its benefits and challenges.

Going through this process by yourself will be suitable if you've always preferred discovering things and gaining new knowledge alone. Some people just like experiencing the thrill of new discoveries and success by themselves. If this is you, then allow your writing medium – your journal, diary, or computer – to be your silent partner throughout this process. Going at it alone just means that no one has to read what you will write; it doesn't mean that you won't ever talk to someone when good things start happening. When amazing things start happening, you may find it irresistible to shut up about it and not talk to your loved ones or friends about it.

If you decide to go through this process with a partner, it is important that you choose someone you trust implicitly, someone who genuinely cares for you, and who will not judge you and who you won't judge, whatever you read in each other's lists. This person may or may not be a spouse, partner or even family member. Sometimes, it is those who are closest to us who show doubt, cynicism and lack of faith when they find out about the miracle we are asking for.

Technique Five: Gratitude Listing

Before you start the 40-day process, it might be worthwhile to agree with your partner on some rules on how you will work together. Set some parameters on things you will accept (for instance, sending your lists any day or time during the week; not commenting on what is on the other person's list unless asked) and won't accept (for example, sending lists on weekends or Sundays; commenting on an item in the other person's list; giving unsolicited advice; asking to discuss things or offering help to the other person).

Having a partner can amplify the effects of what you write in the next 40 days. As you see things developing and favorable breaks start coming your way, it will be exciting to share all this with a partner. Like a gym buddy, he or she can encourage you to continue with the process until you get what you're asking for, or "spot you" when things are starting to feel too heavy to lift and you are tempted to give up on your miracle. He or she can be your source of accountability to remind you of your commitment to see this process through until the end.

Step 4: Decide on a method of recording and communication.

Whether you're doing this technique alone or with a partner, choose a method of recording your lists and communicating them to each other. As for sharing your lists, the state of the internet today, specifically cloud-based applications, allows for dozens of ways you can securely and privately share information with someone. As of the time of this writing, Slack, a cloud-based set of collaboration tools, has become very popular among tech-savvy people as a way to send, receive and keep track of information. Facebook messenger, WhatsApp or other similar apps are also popular alternatives. Make the process of sharing your lists something fun and that each of you will look forward to.

- An even more fun way to share your lists would be to record voice messages on WhatsApp and send them to each other; this allows your partner to listen to your message at the right time and also leaves a chronological audio record of all the lists you send to each other. Don't get bogged down by the actual method you use – email your lists to each other or call each other on the phone and read out your lists if these work for you. Regardless of your chosen communication and sharing method, remember the following requirements:

- One: It is indispensable that – you guessed it – each of you must write down your own lists and keep them.

Although you can speak to your partner and read your list to him or her, you yourself must actually write down your list. It's not enough to think about it because you only keep it in your head if you do and you might also forget about it. Writing your list brings your thoughts outside of you and records them some place where you can easily refer back any day. Your writing can show you how you've grown and developed inwardly during the 40-day period and how the simple act of writing can profoundly affect what's happening in your world. Later on, when you get what you asked for, this written record will be your evidence, plain and objective, that you can create miracles.

- Two: If possible, write your list within 15 to 30 minutes after you wake up in the morning or the same period before you sleep at night.

Endeavor to make it your first act upon waking up or the last act before you sleep the writing of your list. This quarter to half hour period right after you wake up or before you fall asleep is the period when the outpouring of the subconscious mind is at its strongest and when the conscious mind (which is the source of logical thinking and which can analyze or object to whatever it is you are writing) has still not fully awakened. I discuss this in more depth in *Chapter 6 Superconscious Writing*. Melody Beattie also explains that the time right after we wake up is when our real selves are operating, when we're most honest, open and vulnerable, and when we haven't yet activated our denial systems.

Sometimes, however, due to work or family commitments, it is impossible for us to set aside a 15 to 30-minute window to write. You could either solve this by waking up half an hour earlier each day or write before you go to bed when the dishes have been washed, the kids have been tucked in bed and you've kissed your partner good night. You could also keep your journal or diary nearby, open a cloud document if you're in front of a computer at work, or even use your phone and add to your list during the day. As things happen and feelings surface, write about them during the day. If something amazing happens, record it; if something bad happens, write about it too.

- Three: If you're going through this process by yourself, you must ensure that no one else will see, even accidentally, what you write.

If you are doing this with a partner, choose a secure method of information sharing to ensure that only the two of you can read what you send each other.

Step 5: Each morning or night, list what you are grateful for.

This step lies at the core of the 40-day miracle technique. It is what makes this technique work. On your journal or blank document if you're using a word processor, write or type on top of the page, "today I am grateful for/that". Or if you prefer, you can also write, "Thank you for/that" and then write your list.

No doubt you've read about keeping gratitude lists, about writing down every night five or ten things you're grateful for in your life. Counting blessings is good. And you should definitely write down the things you're grateful for in your list. This step, however, goes beyond listing our blessings or writing only about what is good or favorable in our lives. You must also write about the people, events, things and circumstances as well as any associated feelings that you are *least grateful for.* This includes any negative emotions that you are trying to suppress but just can't, or which you are experiencing guilt over for feeling, or which you are trying hard to resist and change. It can also include anything happening in your life or world that has upset, angered, or offended you, which has upset your peace of mind, or which you simply don't like. If anything comes up that you judge as bad or negative, include that in your list as well. Don't edit or censor yourself. Write on your list exactly how you this thing makes you feel. Don't force yourself to be grateful for anything either if you are not ready to do so.

I can almost hear you saying, "What? You mean I should be grateful for the bad stuff happening in my life, things that make me feel bad and downright ungrateful and actually write them down?" Please hear me out.

People or organizations that have hurt or offended us, or circumstances that have happened to us that we deem unfair or unjust, and which create resentment in us are the perfect things to include on your list. Resentment, and its correlates, anger, rage, bitterness, jealousy, and hatred could be the very emotions that are blocking and preventing your good, the miracle that you've been asking for, from coming to you and you receiving it. By writing them down, you allow yourself to release these stuck emotions and clear the way for you to begin experiencing the good, positive emotions that you desire to have.

For you, there really might be occasions, events, circumstances of situations for which it would be inappropriate or wrong to feel gratitude. Some things are truly off-limits. For instance, it would inappropriate and downright wrong to feel grateful for the death of a loved one or for having a serious or terminal illness and to write, "I'm thankful for that". If you believe in God or a higher power, it will just be wrong and taking their name in vain to thank them for an unfortunate event like the death of a child. I believe, though, that any situation, no matter how seemingly bad or unfortunate on the surface, carries the seed of something good.

Good can be born even from the most serious misfortunes. And you can always find another way to approach these bad or unfortunate events. You could write that you're grateful for what your loved one who has passed away means to you, how much you miss them, and how you wish you could change certain things that happened between you and them. Instead of writing "I'm grateful to have learned that I have a serious illness", you could write, "I'm grateful that help is on the way" or "I'm thankful for the day when I am well again". Instead of being grateful that you have no job and no money, or are alone, you could give thanks that the right job, the money, or the right person is on the way. Instead of focusing on your current situation, you could always look toward the good that you hope will come, and write how grateful you are for that.

In your list, you can include a list of things that you desire to get or events that you would like to happen or outcomes you would like to achieve in the future, and be grateful for them in advance. If you don't know what to do next regarding a situation, circumstance, event or relationship, and are feeling confused and in need of guidance (like I was when I first did this technique) or are feeling stuck in your life, then you could list down exactly what you need right now and write that you're thankful that you will receive what you need or have asked for. Don't hesitate or be scared to ask for what you really want. While you're already asking, you might as well ask big.

Step 6: For each item on your list, briefly state why you are grateful for it.

If you're going through this process with a partner, there's no need to explain to him or her the entire background or for them to understand exactly what's going on with you. Assuming you've given each other permission at the start to clarify each other's lists, they can always ask you about a specific thing you've listed. You can write speculatively, such as, "I'm grateful that this event has happened" or "I'm grateful I've received this thing because I believe it will allow this other event to happen or for me to receive this other thing".

Step 7: List down the people you resent, who have wronged or offended you and who you can't forgive or haven't forgiven.

This follows-on from Step 5, but is the second most important step and deserves a paragraph of its own.

I wrote above how resentment and its correlates anger, bitterness, rage, hatred, are debilitating and, ultimately, destructive emotions. They will block the good that you sometimes so desperately seek, from coming to you. Melody Beattie in *Miracles* expressed it best when she wrote: "Having a heart blocked with resentments is the number one barrier, according to many experts, to achieving what we want in life, to manifesting our goals, and to experiencing joy."

Technique Five: Gratitude Listing

I know that forgiving someone who has really hurt you is easier said than done. But make no mistake: ultimately you must forgive everyone. Universal law mandates that we must forgive if we want to be forgiven.

Fortunately, through your writing, there are two ways that you can begin to forgive someone even if every cell in your body screams "never!" I believe this is one of the most sublimely miraculous attributes of writing – its healing ability.

The first way is to include the way you exactly feel toward these people, organizations, institutions, corporations, events and circumstances on your gratitude list. At this stage, you don't even have to feel any inclination toward forgiving this person or entity; following step 5, just write, "today, I am grateful for the anger, hurt, bitterness or resentment that I feel toward this person (or entity)". Then, following step 6, write a brief description of why you feel this way toward this person or entity.

If you wish, you can also describe anything positive at all that has come from your resentment or anger; anything positive will do (for example, "I am grateful that I am so angry at this person that I now no longer talk to them and have stopped communicating with them; I get so upset whenever I see them, at least now, I don't have to be as upset because I'm no longer in contact with them"). You can even write, "I'm grateful that I can't forgive this person at this stage because I need time to process and think about what has happened."

In the coming days, you might notice the pattern of your writing start to change. For instance, you might start writing, "Even though I still feel betrayed and hurt by what this person has done, still I'm grateful that at one point in my life, we did share some good times" or you might write "I'm still grateful that this person was able to help me in some specific way". You'll also begin to notice that accompanying this shift in your writing is a perceptible releasing of your negative feelings; it doesn't feel as bad anymore when you write about this person or entity. Just allow this gradual shifting in your writing to continue. Then when you are ready, try the second way: actually write, "today, I am grateful that I am ready to forgive this person and move on with my life," or you could even write, "today I am grateful that I have forgiven this person."

You don't even have to actually feel genuine gratitude at this point for what you're writing. Recall from *Chapter 1 Mind your Energy* that writing is a psychoneuromotor activity. This means that merely performing the physical act of writing can direct your thoughts and consequently unlock your feelings. What is important is that you have begun to release the poisonous build-up of negative feelings within you. If you keep writing in this way, I promise you that genuine forgiveness will eventually come. It may take a while, but your heart will one day be free.

Key points to remember

Throughout the 40 days, do not over-think, or intellectualize this process. For step 5 in particular, don't over-analyze, judge, censor or edit what you write in your list. Let everything out.

Allow time for things to develop. There will be days when you feel super-charged as you write your list and you truly feel excited, appreciative and grateful for every item on that list; on these days, write more! And squeeze out every ounce of gratitude you can for the good things happening to you. I guarantee, though, that there will be days when it feels like there is absolutely nothing to be grateful for; it is especially on these days that you must write. Make a commitment to complete the 40 days and follow through.

With regard to step 7 in particular, give yourself time. Some things, like releasing pent up or deep-seated negative emotions, will take time. Many of us have been burdened by the debilitating

Technique Five: Gratitude Listing

effects of these negative emotions for as long as we can recall. Unfortunately, there is no way to rush this: it may take months, even years for resentment, anger, or bitterness to become unblocked; and years for hurt and betrayal to be finally released. And if you succeed in doing this, and the way is now clear for your good to come to you, it still might take time for it to actually appear in your world. So, take all the time that you need. If you persist, fortunately, the rewards – freedom to finally let all your good in or the appearance of the miracle you've asked for – is well worth the effort and wait.

As with all the techniques that I've shared in this book, adapt the 40-day miracle technique to fit your own needs, situation and circumstances.

Technique Six: Superconscious Writing

Downloading from the Universal Supercomputer

"I was going through a really difficult time around the autumn of 1968," Paul McCartney said in an interview. The world-famous musician and ex-Beatle was referring to the time late in the band's career, when they had begun making a follow-up album to the "White Album".

"As a group we were starting to have problems," Paul explained. "I think I was sensing the Beatles were breaking up, so I was staying up late at night, drinking, doing drugs, clubbing, the way a lot of people were at the time. I was really living and playing hard." By then, the other three Beatles were already living in the country with their partners, while Paul was still alone, a bachelor still living in London. He wondered whether it was about time he found someone (this was shortly before he met his first wife Linda).

"I think I was getting, like, a little bit over the top with the whole thing – getting pretty tired and pretty wasted," he added. One night, Paul went to bed and had a restless sleep. He described what happened next. "Somewhere between deep sleep and insomnia, I had the most comforting dream about my mother." Paul's mother, Mary, died when he was 14 years old and had been dead for about 10 years when he dreamed about her that night. "It was as if she could see that I was troubled. There was her face, completely clear, particularly her eyes, and she said to me very gently, very reassuringly: 'It's going to be ok. Don't worry. Let it be. Let it be.''

Paul recounted that he woke up with a great feeling as he remembered the dream. "It was really like she had visited me at this very difficult point in my life and gave me this message: be gentle, don't fight things, just try and go with the flow and it will all work out." Being a musician, Paul did what came naturally. He wrote a song using the same feeling from the dream and of his mother coming to him in the dream. "I went right over to the piano and started writing a song: "When I find myself in times of trouble, Mother Mary comes to me. Speaking words of wisdom, let it be. There will be an answer, let it be."

It didn't take long for him to finish writing the song. The song that came to Paul McCartney when he was unconscious, in a moment of peace and calm while in the sleep state, would go on to become one of the most famous songs of the 20th century.

Abnormal breakthroughs

'Let it be' was not Paul McCartney's only experience of receiving inspiration from a dream. The tune for 'Yesterday', which arguably tops even 'Let it be' as the most famous song of the 20th century, came to him – complete – in a dream.

How is it that some people, like Paul McCartney, are able to access inspiration from a hidden inexhaustible source of creative energy that allows them to create amazing things like songs, plays, poems, designs, inventions, computer algorithms that impact the world forever? Why is it that some people, at the most ordinary moments, receive an unexpected revelation from somewhere outside of them, from some kind of intelligence or power higher than their own, that allows them to generate concepts and ideas that alter the course of human history?

Consider these other examples from the creative arts:

Mozart could visualize an entire opera in his mind, note perfect, before he started writing. He wrote down these visualizations, often writing first – and final – drafts of an entire opera from his mind. There were no mistakes in the score, no need for revisions and it was ready to be played in public.

Beethoven created some of his greatest works, including the entire Ninth Symphony, when he was already almost totally deaf.

Stephen Hawking was so crippled with Lou Gehrig's disease that he needed a special computer to speak. Yet it was no obstacle for him to write his beautifully complex book, *A Brief History of Time.*

Shakespeare actually adopted ideas from other people's plays for his own plays. But he didn't simply derive his plays from those other works; he blended them with his real-life experiences into something fresh and new.

There are many other examples of people who accessed some mysterious reserve of knowledge and wisdom to powerfully change the world for the better.

Thomas Edison, one of the greatest inventors who ever lived, who patented more than a thousand devices, regularly took naps during the day to access this font of knowledge to solve seemingly unsolvable problems. As a result, he achieved historic breakthroughs in electricity, motion pictures, sound recording and transmission, and hundreds of other areas.

Molecular biologist James Watson, with his partner Francis Crick, discovered the double helix – the twisted ladder-like structure of DNA – in a flash of inspiration while shifting around cardboard cut-outs of the bases of DNA on his office table. Their discovery is the basis of today's genetic engineering and gene sequencing, as well as the billion-dollar biotechnology industry.

The idea for Google came to company co-founder Larry Page, when he was a 22-year-old Stanford graduate student. He dreamed (dreams again!) the basis of an algorithm to download the entire World Wide Web and examine the links between the pages. He wrote it down when he awoke and the concept worked. He called it PageRank and used it to power a search engine initially named BackRub, which was later fortunately re-named Google.

The idea for the Periodic Table of Elements, which is the basis of modern chemistry, was dreamed (and dreams yet again!) by 19th century chemist Dmitri Mendeleev. Before him, no other scientist had been able to connect all the elements together in a single table that correlated with all their properties. In sleep, Mendeleev saw in a dream a table where all elements fell into place as required. Of this experience, he said; "awakening, I immediately wrote (the idea) down on a piece of paper". The idea came to him almost perfect; in fact, after writing it down, only in one place did a correction seem necessary.

There are so many other examples I could give you. What allowed these people to seemingly stumble upon these amazing ideas, which all came at apparently random times, and most often in dreams during sleep? Is it because these people were born special, with qualities and mental abilities not possessed by the rest of us, "normal" humans?

I don't believe this, not for one moment. In your own life, you must have also experienced similar flashes of brilliant inspiration that solved a perplexing problem or showed the way out of a complex dilemma. Your flashes may not have led to earth-shaking, history-altering discoveries; yet I have no doubt that they were as momentous or life-changing for you. If you've had these experiences, the same as these more famous people I listed, then it means that it's something that all human beings can have.

What is common in these stories of famous discoveries, and perhaps also in your own similar stories, is that these sudden bursts of clarity, knowledge and inspiration, seem to come from somewhere outside of the people who received them; they couldn't have come up with these ideas themselves, at least not by doing what they had been regularly doing up to that point.

These flashes of brilliance do not come randomly or by accident. They can be prompted whenever we want. They come from an always-accessible source of knowledge and inspiration available to all humans.

This source is the Superconscious Mind.

Collective Unconscious or Infinite Intelligence?

I have done much research and read a lot of available literature on the Superconscious Mind, in the hopes of actually defining what it is. But I'll be honest with you: it is impossible to define. It's the same with other mysterious concepts like the subconscious mind, black holes, dark matter and dark energy. We know they exist; we can prove they exist. But no one knows exactly what they are. In the case of the Superconscious Mind, we know it exists because of the countless experiences of people as I've described above. Knowing it exists is one thing; defining it is another.

People have variously named the Superconscious Mind as Infinite Intelligence, the Universal supercomputer, the Collective Unconscious, the Mind of God, and many others. It's not easy to pin a definitive label on the Superconscious mind.

Fortunately, it's much easier to describe how it works and how to activate it. Again, it's similar to other concepts, like electricity or gravity for instance. Not too many people can describe with scientific accuracy what electricity or gravity are or exactly how they work. But it's easy to describe how they work practically and how to activate or benefit from them. With electricity, it powers all our appliances, gives us light, warms us and allows us to cook our food. To activate it, you just plug an appliance into a wall socket. With gravity, it allows us to fly planes, draw water from an elevated level, or play any game involving a rubber ball. To experience it, just jump (but not too high!) or play tennis or basketball.

Can you actually see the Superconscious Mind in operation? Gravity is invisible but it's easy to see when it's working. Just release an object from any height. But you can't see the same thing with the Superconscious Mind. You can't see the Mind of God, right? Or can you?

Have you ever seen a school of fish move underwater? It's the most amazing sight: a swimming, whirling, swirling spherical mass composed of thousands of distinct, independent tiny creatures moving as one body. Scientists explain that fish swim in schools to better protect themselves from predators, improve their foraging and swim more efficiently. But this doesn't explain how they can swim this way.

Have you given a second thought about how geese and other birds are able to navigate up to 50,000 miles every year as they migrate between their summer and winter grounds? They don't have GPS systems, maps or a compass like humans do. Yet they travel the same course year after year with little deviation and always find their way to their destination halfway around the world. The secrets of birds' amazing navigational skills aren't fully understood even by scientists.

There is no mystery behind these phenomena. This is the Superconscious Mind at work guiding the fish and birds. And it is

Technique Six: Superconscious Writing

constantly guiding us humans too; except that most of the time we are unaware of this guidance or how to tap into it.

The Superconscious Mind is the most powerful faculty that has ever been discovered in human experience. It's like a universal supercomputer that you can access to answer questions or deal with problems that you could not hope to answer or manage yourself. To activate it, you must ask a question of or seek answers, information or knowledge from it. You do this when you are relaxed, centered and calm, preferably in meditation or during sleep. Give the superconscious time to give you the answer, information or knowledge you seek. And when it comes, you write down what has been revealed to you. If you are required or prompted to take some kind of action arising from the answer you receive, do it.

The Superconscious Mind also seems to respond best when you direct written questions or requests for answers and knowledge from it. In this chapter, I'll teach several proven writing techniques to help you access the Superconscious Mind.

Nature of the thing

Humans have known about and discussed the Superconscious Mind for millennia. But for majority of this time, knowing about the Superconscious Mind was considered secret, even mystical knowledge. In ancient times, it was usually reserved for masters, wise men and mystics. To learn their knowledge, a student had to study many years under teachers of the mystical schools. It has only been relatively recently, perhaps the last century, that the Superconscious Mind has been demystified and knowledge of its workings made more available; but even then, only a few individuals learned this knowledge, and still fewer people actually practiced it.

In 1895, Sigmund Freud, the founder of psychotherapy, described the three minds—the ego, id and superego. He described them as three different elements of perception and would later base much of his work on them.

The ego is the Conscious Mind. It is the part of the mind that is alert and aware, which deals with the external world and can analyze, decide and take action. We refer to this part of the mind when we say "I am".

The id is the Subconscious Mind. It is the repository of all our memories and feelings, the vast storehouse where all the thoughts, decisions and experiences we've ever had in our lives are kept. Unlike the ego, the id functions automatically and independently of our conscious awareness; it operates our bodies and aligns our thoughts and feelings with past experiences.

The superego is the third dimension of the mind. It has been called many names by different experts—"oversoul" (Ralph Waldo Emerson); "collective unconscious" (Alfred Adler, a student of Freud); "supra conscious" (Carl Jung); "infinite intelligence" (Napoleon Hill); "Superconscious Mind" or "God Mind" (Roberto Assagioli, Italian psychologist); and "thinking stuff" (Wallace Wattles).

The Superconscious Mind has been called many names by people. Whatever you call it, it remains to be the great universal power that you can access any time. You can seek its aid to help you achieve any goal that you intensely desire.

Whispers and Eureka moments

As shown in the stories above, the Superconscious Mind has been responsible for many amazing human breakthroughs. Brian Tracy, in his book *Goals!* even goes as far as saying that all important breakthroughs in all fields of human endeavor throughout history have been the result of superconscious functioning. He describes it as perhaps the most important mental law ever discovered. It is the true source of any great or inspiring work of art, classic piece of literature, sublimely-beautiful poem or extraordinary piece of music. It has inspired builders with the ideas for remarkable buildings and structures.

Even in the realms of money and finance, individuals have credited the operation of the superconscious mind as inspiring ideas that brought massive wealth. Napoleon Hill, author of arguably the most famous self-development book of the 20th century, *Think and Grow Rich,* who interviewed many millionaires in researching for his book, found that virtually all of the most successful people in America accessed the superconscious mind continually throughout their careers. These individuals credit it as the source of all their most important breakthroughs and achievements.

You need not be a Shakespeare, Mozart or Edison to experience the mysterious and potent operation of the superconscious mind. I am certain that you've had several experiences of the superconscious mind at work, but you just weren't aware of it. Recall your experiences. Whenever you suddenly came up with a brilliant idea or insight that solved a problem or showed the way out of a dilemma, I'll bet you had a superconscious experience.

When the Superconscious Mind strikes you with a flash of inspiration, you are left without a doubt that you've been hit by something that you didn't create or cause on your own. If you've ever had an experience like this (and I'm certain you've had at least one in your life) then you know the feeling I'm referring to. It's a "eureka" moment. In fact, the word eureka is now synonymous with the arrival of superconscious insight. Translated from the original Greek, "eureka" means "I have found it!" The Greek mathematician and physicist Archimedes is said to have yelled it when he was struck by a superconscious flash of inspiration about the displacement of objects while sitting in his bath.

So, superconscious moments certainly often come to people in Archimedes-like "eureka" moments. But in my own experience, superconscious moments don't always come as bolts of lightning; they don't always electrify you with their brilliance. They have also come to me in subtle ways, through my intuition. The intuition is our link to the Superconscious Mind and so for that reason we should pay close attention to its promptings. I definitely agree with Brian Tracy when he wrote that sometimes our intuition will speak so loudly to us in the silence that the inspiration or insight it brings us is life-changing.

I still remember superconscious moments that have come to me in my life. One of them prompted me to write this book. I was sitting at a street market, where my partner Antonella had set up shop for the day to sell her homemade Italian biscuits and cakes. I had brought a book—*Goals!* by Brian Tracy—to read and while away the time as Antonella sold her food. It was an uneventful morning, no different from other mornings spent at the street market. I was reading from the book and learning some pretty amazing things about how to set goals and achieve them. I thought the book was teaching me some valuable lessons and it was great that many others could learn from it too. And then a thought zapped my mind: it came so suddenly and without warning that "zapped" is the only word I can think of to describe it. "Write a book about writing techniques that have helped you solve problems, achieve goals and transform your life." This was the definite thought that came to me. Not only that—the exact contents of the book came simultaneously with the arrival of this thought. I remember looking at the table of contents of the book I was holding at that moment and I could also see the table of contents of my own imaginary book virtually complete.

I have had similar experiences like this before, but not many. I had never written a full non-fiction book before. I had previously

Technique Six: Superconscious Writing

self-published a fiction book, but it never occurred to me, nor was I particularly interested, to write a non-fiction, self-development book. I was a big fan of the self-development genre and owned some of the most famous titles in this genre, but I never had any burning desire to write one myself. Never, that is until that moment at the street market. And the idea came so suddenly, completely and fully formed that it reminded me of a scene from the movie Amadeus. In that scene, an adult Mozart, who was at the apex of his musical powers, was asked by an agitated patron who had commissioned him to write an opera and been kept waiting by the eccentric composer, "where's my opera?" To which Mozart replied, "it's all right here in my head. The rest is just scribbling."

I was so happy and excited about what had just happened that I couldn't wait to start writing the book. As Mozart had said, the book was already complete in my head, I had just to scribble the words on paper. All this convinced me that the idea that zapped my mind that day did not come from me, but from elsewhere. I didn't know from where exactly, but it sure wasn't from me. I didn't have a name for it then, but I had just had a rare superconscious idea.

Through my research, I would later discover that a superconscious idea or answer possesses three qualities.

- First: it will answer every aspect of a problem you ask it to solve or provide all that you need to accomplish your goal. The solution or idea will be complete in every respect. It will also feel natural, easy and exactly right for the situation.

- Second: it will come as a blazing flash of insight. Its arrival might come suddenly and unexpectedly, but the idea it brings might seem so obvious that you knock your head thinking why you had never thought of it before.

- Third: a superconscious idea or answer is accompanied by a rush of excitement and exhilaration. You will feel energized and will want to start working on the idea right away. Above all, you will feel happy at having been given this idea.

Getting a superconscious idea was an unforgettable moment for me, as I am sure it was for those people whose stories I related above. As I am sure it will be for you.

Awakening

Here are some first principles to remember before I talk about how to access the Superconscious Mind.

- Principle 1: Any thought, plan, goal or idea held continuously in the conscious mind must inevitably, and in due course, be brought into reality by the Superconscious Mind.

- Principle 2: Any goal that is written down, continuously desired and consistently acted on with deliberate intention, will impress and elicit the aid of the Superconscious Mind.

- Principle 3: Any thought, plan, goal or idea held continuously in the conscious mind and acted upon with inspired action will be impressed upon the Superconscious Mind.

Technique Six: Superconscious Writing

The Superconscious Mind is most accessible when your mind is calm, relaxed and peaceful. As I described in *Chapter 1 Mind Your Energy*, this state can also be described as the feeling of being "centered". Different authors have expressed this same thought in different ways. Joseph Murphy, who wrote *The Power of Your Subconscious Mind*, explained that this higher intelligence can be easily accessed when we put ourselves in a sleepy, drowsy state (without actually falling asleep). Neville Goddard, author of *The Law and the Promise*, wrote along similar lines; he explained that to tap into this higher, creative force, we begin by inducing a state akin to sleep. This is why one technique he taught was to visualize your goal and imagine what it would feel like if it were already fulfilled, just prior to falling asleep. Brian Tracy recommends practicing relaxation in solitude, completely letting go of all your cares and sitting quietly or communicating with nature.

Clearly, what is common in all of these techniques is the requirement of silence. We need to be silent as we place ourselves in the presence of superconscious intelligence. I personally believe that superconscious intelligence speaks to us all the time, but we do not hear it most of the time because we are not silent. And if we are not silent, we cannot listen. Consider this for a moment: "silent" is actually an anagram of "listen". It is by being silent that we open ourselves to the voice of the Superconscious Mind.

A major block to our hearing the inner guidance of the Superconscious Mind is all the "noise" in our heads – uncontrolled, and often unwanted voices, thoughts, images and concepts that obstruct the clear reception of impressions from the Superconscious Mind. Our minds are naturally restless; this is caused by mental noise, often in the form of negative, destructive self-talk. The Superconscious Mind is often easily accessible via our intuition. But all this mental noise blocks our intuition.

So, it is necessary that we silence our mental noise and self-talk; only then will it be possible for the messages from the Superconscious Mind to be received by our subconscious mind and for the subconscious mind to bring that message to our conscious minds.

The other reason behind the requirement of silence is that when we go through a regular, normal day, it is our conscious mind that operates. This is our default state. Author Grant Hudson explains that our conscious mind is not directly linked with the Superconscious Mind (or what he called the "collective knowledge base"). For this reason, we cannot easily access it during our normal waking hours.

It is our subconscious minds that are directly linked to the Superconscious Mind. It is our subconscious mind that is able to download this information from the Superconscious Mind. And if we know how, we can bring what the subconscious mind has received into our conscious awareness.

Grant Hudson has a simple and clear explanation for how the creative process involving the three minds works:

Step 1: you desire something and with the proper tools you impress that idea into your subconscious mind.

Step 2: now your subconscious mind taps into the unlimited database of the universe and receives the needed information.

Step 3: once you have it in your subconscious mind, it either comes to your conscious awareness like a sudden realization or you will have to deliberately work to bring it to your awareness using certain techniques.

Thereafter, if you trust the Superconscious Mind and act on that idea, you will be astounded by the results.

Technique Six: Superconscious Writing

This process is not a secret. Yet despite this simple process, thousands of people fail at the last particular step. Why? The reason is the fear of taking action.

When you use the writing techniques I will teach in the next part, you will soon, maybe even immediately, receive ideas. Regardless of whether you've totally figured out what the idea is or you're not sure about it, you must take action. Implement the idea. Execute the plan that you've been presented with. And soon, with practice, you will become more adept at listening to and hearing the voice of the Superconscious Mind.

Downloading

Inspired guidance from the Superconscious Mind is always flowing to us. If we want to receive these impressions then we have to clear the communication channels through which the Superconscious Mind moves. We have to ready our minds to download this information. In general, this can be achieved through imagination and meditation.

"The power of imagination makes us infinite," said Scottish-American naturalist and author John Muir. Imagination is the thread that links our conscious and subconscious minds and the infinite, Superconscious Mind. The use of imagination is most often associated with artists like writers, composers and designers. They feel a creative impulse and are able to imagine that impulse into being; they then harness inspiration to bring to life what they have imagined, and capture this in their chosen media, be it words, music or designs.

It's not difficult to distinguish ideas that come from the Superconscious Mind from those that come from our own conscious minds. Ideas from the Superconscious Mind usually come in the form of a truly creative idea. Writers and artists who access the

Superconscious Mind often experience this. But truly creative ideas are not the exclusive domain of writers and other artists; anyone can have these creative, inspired ideas when they link with the Superconscious Mind.

Imagination is often best combined with meditation. By meditation, I do not mean any spiritual or religious practice. Stripped of these connotations, meditation refers simply to the act of paying attention to only one thing. You can do this either as a spiritual or religious activity or as a way of becoming calm or relaxed. Meditation stills the mind and quiets the obstructive mental noise. As a result, we are better able to receive impressions from the superconscious mind.

Try it yourself: Superconscious Writing

A proven way to access the Superconscious Mind is through writing. The Superconscious Mind is ready, willing and able to give you thoughts, ideas and inspiration to assist you to accomplish any sincere, honest and worthwhile objective. Your objective could be to achieve a big goal or solve a perplexing problem.

In *Goals!* Brian Tracy succinctly summarized the process of activating the Superconscious Mind toward the achievement of a worthwhile objective. He wrote: "The Superconscious Mind is activated by clear, specific and written goals, intensely desired, visualized regularly, and constantly worked toward."

As I wrote above, your starting point must be to center, relax and calm yourself. While in this state, begin to visualize and put emotional content in a specific result that you desire intensely. This state stimulates the Superconscious Mind into giving you ideas and energy for the attainment of your objective.

Try these two following techniques to tap into the Superconscious Mind.

Technique Six: Superconscious Writing

Writing in white heat

In college, my freshman English composition teacher, Mrs Lacuesta, gave one piece of advice that I haven't forgotten even though I heard it 25 years ago:

Write in white heat. Edit in cold blood.

She gave this advice in the context of artistic, creative writing. In other words, when you write anything creative, for example a scene in a play, chapter in a book, poem or song, let yourself go. Write like your brain is on fire with ideas and your hands can't write fast enough to capture the ideas the brain is feeding them. Before you write, relax, take a few deep breaths, and let the ideas flow. No matter if only one idea forms in your mind. If you let your mind wander, I guarantee more ideas will come. Since I heard this advice, this is how I have always started any creative piece of writing.

As I explained in Chapter 1, thoughts are sometimes like links in a never-ending chain. As soon as you think of one thought, if you don't stop your mind from moving, then another thought will link to that thought, and another one will link to that. And the thoughts won't stop until you tell them to. When you're trying to write a story for example, don't cut, censor or edit your thoughts. If you write like your brain is on fire, then ideas will shoot from it like sparks. Keep recording those sparks until the fire starts to cool down. After the fire has died down, you can come back and see what you've created. Now you can edit, cut and change things around.

Even though this advice was given during a class on fiction writing, it applies just as well to any of the four types of writing that this book teaches. It works particularly well though when you are writing to co-create or achieve a goal or an objective and when you are writing to receive answers and guidance or solve problems. Your mind is capable of generating thousands of ideas to help you achieve an objective. But there is an infinite, uncountable, number of ideas stored in your subconscious mind. We are looking for the one or two ideas in there that have come from the Superconscious Mind. This is the real good stuff. If you develop these ideas and later act on them, it will launch your goal setting or problem solving to a whole new level.

Here are the steps to writing in white heat:

First: relax, calm and center yourself.

Put yourself in a condition to receive impressions from the Superconscious Mind. Imagine as if the Superconscious Mind will speak to you through the voice of a small child. The words will be few and simple. You will pick them up right away. But her voice might be faint, like a whisper, so you really have to pay attention, else you might miss what was said. (Re-read Chapter 1 for more guidance on calming yourself before writing.)

Second: be ready to write.

You need to be able to record the ideas and answers when they come. Take a notebook or piece of paper and pen. Or open a new word document or whatever writing app you use. One student of mine composes a new email and after sends it to God or the Universe (and she's even created a real receiving email account for it too!).

Third: set a time limit.

Allot 5 or 10 minutes for writing non-stop or "in white heat". You can choose whatever time suits you. But as we will be attempting to write while our minds are in burning white, as opposed to cooling down reddish heat, I suggest don't set this time limit too long (15 minutes might be ok, but half an hour could be too long).

Fourth: pose a specific question to your Superconscious Mind.

Imagine you are asking this question and that you're addressing it to the Superconscious Mind who can hear you. This step is not meant to be spiritual or religious in any way. But if it helps you, you can picture the Superconscious Mind as God, Buddha, Allah or any other figure you revere, or even a loved one like a parent or relative. If it helps too, ask your question as if you're asking a specific person.

For example, if you're in goal setting mode, ask and write: "Superconscious mind, tell me how I can… (insert adverb here: quickly, completely, efficiently, easily, etc) achieve, accomplish, reach, do…(insert specific goal here).

If you're in problem solving mode, ask and write, "Superconscious mind, how can I…(again insert adverb here) fix, solve, address, overcome, hurdle, win…(then insert specific issue or problem here).

Fifth: write in white heat.

During the allotted time, write non-stop every single idea and detail that comes to you. Have you ever seen movies showing a medium or psychic doing automatic writing? It looks like they're not aware of what they're doing but their hands are moving like crazy, scribbling, writing words on paper. Sometimes the writing is so fast that the words come out almost as unintelligible scribbles and another person has to be there to quickly pull out the sheet of paper the medium is writing on so she can write on a fresh piece of paper.

This is kind of how writing in white heat looks to me. Write fast and do not linger on a page. There will be times when an idea will pop up in your head and you'll think it's ridiculous, even crazy and will never work. This is just your conscious and rational mind thinking this. You must write especially these ideas, because you have no way of knowing at this point if this idea is the superconscious one.

Sixth. leave it alone.

After blazing through the list of all possible ways of getting your goal or solving your problem, leave your list and come back to it after some time has passed. Then, like a fisherman checking his nets if he caught the one elusive fish that he was waiting for or like a prospector patiently sifting the water in his pan and waiting to see that sudden flash in it that could signal the presence of gold, check your list for the superconscious idea or solution. Then you can proceed to organize your ideas in terms of what's doable or feasible right now, which ones you can do later, and which ones to completely eliminate. Read *Chapter 4 GoalSeek* and *Chapter 8 Vision Mapping* on how to use your writing to organize a plan for achieving your goals.

Evening and Morning Pages

This technique can be used on its own or in conjunction with writing in white heat.

The subconscious mind is the link between our conscious, rational-thinking mind and the infinite Superconscious Mind. It's critical then that you tune in to what your subconscious mind is telling you.

How do you know what you want? How do you know what your goals are? How can you sift through a whole slew of ideas to know which ones are important? The subconscious can answer all these questions. And it can speak to us in many ways.

Technique Six: Superconscious Writing

If you are not sure what you want, let alone how to get there from here, let your writing help point you to the path you're meant to follow.

Early morning is a perfect time for crystallizing your desires. Set the alarm clock 15-20 minutes before you ordinarily rise and start writing as soon as you wake up. Bring the pad and the pen right into bed with you, so you're ready to write once you awake.

Write sleepy, twilight-zone thoughts. Write about the irritation in your eyes if they hurt. If you wish you could go back to sleep, write about that. These are "warm up," stretching motions before the exercise begins in earnest, because after you run out of things to complain about, your pen moves on and starts giving you some useful direction. Do this faithfully for two weeks without re-reading what you wrote, and then, at the end of the two weeks, read it over and notice any pattern.

If you are an evening person, you can write before going to sleep at night. Thomas Edison used sleep to get creative insights from the Superconscious Mind. He even took regular naps during the day for this purpose. He said that he never went to sleep without sending a request to this mind. When he awoke, he always wrote down any answers that he received while in slumber.

You will do the same as Edison. Here's a simple routine to get you started: about 15 minutes before you go to bed, meditate on the question you want to ask the Superconscious Mind. Then write down the question on paper. Ask plenty of questions connected with what you're trying to accomplish and note them on paper. As Edison described it, present requests to your subconscious mind. The more specific and detailed your questions, the clearer the answers you will get.

If all that comes out is the same initial question but phrased in different ways, then write just that. Or if some semblance of an answer to the question starts coming, then write that too. Keep writing until you're ready to fall asleep. If nothing comes, don't stress. Go to sleep and trust that the answer will be there in the morning.

When you awake, follow the instructions above on morning pages. While you slept, your subconscious mind was wandering all night, possibly receiving instructions directly from the Superconscious Mind. First thing in the morning, when your conscious mind is clearly attuned, without noise, to your subconscious mind, write down the impressions you get relating to your requests from the previous evening.

Often, the answer will come in the form of a dream. It's important to note that dreams are generated by your subconscious mind so you should note what it's trying to tell you in the form of your dreams. I am not telling you to try and interpret your dream as some sort of prophetic vision. Rather, clue in to the messages that are hidden in your dreams. What you must do is set a strong, deliberate intention to receive answers from the subconscious mind before you sleep. When you awake, write down what you dreamed in a notebook. This way, you will be able to figure out if your subconscious mind was trying to send you the answer through dream imagery.

Through your writing, your subconscious is letting you know what you want. Writing speaks to us and gives us clues, sometimes in roundabout ways. Listen carefully. Use your writing to interpret the symbols.

Final key points

Your Superconscious Mind will bring you the exact answer you need at exactly the right time. It may not be the time you were expecting, but I guarantee the answer will come and not a moment too soon.

Technique Six: Superconscious Writing

What do you do after the Superconscious Mind gives you the answer? How do you proceed when you receive a superconscious inspiration? First you write it down of course! Just like Paul McCartney did, and this is why we now have songs like "Yesterday" and "Let It Be" to sing until the end of time.

Next you should take action immediately. Don't delay. This information is time-stamped and will expire if you delay. If you get an inner prompting to take an action, like make a phone call, move on it quickly. If you have a hunch about something, pursue it. Often, the very act of moving on a superconscious flash will trigger additional superconscious insights and inspirations that will help you.

Learn to distinguish between inspired action and desperate action. You should always take the former and avoid the latter. Inspired action is spurred on by the leading and creative inspiration of the Superconscious Mind. You'll know this type of action because when you do it, there is never any stress, tension or desperation to make things happen. When you're taking inspired action, things feel natural and results flow easily. After taking inspired action, you may feel tired physically but your mind is still buzzing with energy.

When you take inspired action, it doesn't mean that you move slowly though. It has nothing to do with speed but your state of mind when you act and what's causing you to act. In fact, inspired action usually has to be done quickly and efficiently.

On the other hand, desperate action is driven by panic – we do it because we're taking matters completely in our own hands and trying to get results or solve problems our way. You'll know, too, this type of action right away because when you do it, you'll be panicky and feeling stressed. You'll be frantically going from one thing to the next in an effort to keep up. You'll feel desperate, like you're rowing upstream. And even after so much effort, you're not achieving the results you hoped for. After taking desperate action, you'll often feel exhausted physically and mentally.

In applying the techniques of this chapter, or any chapter in WriteTech for that matter, trust and faith are critical. You must trust that the Superconscious Mind will come up with exactly the answer you need or the solution to your plight and that it will come at the right time. If the answer seems delayed, you must have faith that it's coming. Having faith also means being still and at peace. The more you trust in the Superconscious Mind, the more it will open up to you.

And think big. Always think big. Don't be afraid to reach out to the Superconscious Mind. This is the very presence of the divine in your life. Don't be afraid to touch it. Trust that the superconscious will respond to you when you need it to.

Technique Seven: Calling S.O.S. to the Universe

When you need to manifest a solution fast

There are times in life when we might find ourselves facing problems that seem so hopelessly unsolvable or being trapped in trying situations and it's impossible for us, or those near to us, to see any end to the situation or any way we can come out of it unbroken and whole. Sometimes these moments comprise a seemingly endless series of days, weeks, months or even years of waiting, waiting for something to change, to break. The waiting seems endless, pointless and hopeless. And it seems that we are left with no choice but to give up.

It is in moments like these that the Universe calls to us to call out to it for help. We can call out to the Universe through a simple letter. And in a way we can never fathom or explain, the Universe answers.

I encountered this technique of writing to the Universe in the works of Melody Fletcher as well as Henriette Klauser. I have seen and experienced first-hand in my own life and in the lives of others how powerful this technique can be.

Nadia's story

Nadia left home in Valencia, Spain for Australia in 2013. She left Spain because the country was in the midst of a recession and professionals like her could not get work for long stretches of time, sometimes years. Nadia had graduated with an honors bachelors' degree in psychology and also completed a specialization in cognitive psychotherapy. She held dual registrations as a psychologist and psychotherapist in Spain.

She came to Australia by herself, believing that she would be able to find work in her field. She was convinced that someone with her qualifications and experience would certainly, and quickly find work. What followed next was years of waiting.

Until you actually go through an extended period of unemployment, there is no way you can adequately understand or imagine the feelings of pain, hopelessness and despair that someone who has been jobless for a long time feels. Weeks and months of job hunting, sending hundreds of resumes, getting the sporadic phone call from a remotely interested employer, followed by the extremely rare job interview, all end with the loud thud of the letter of rejection.

From November 2013 until November 2018, Nadia didn't get a single job in her field. She wasn't totally jobless – she worked casually as a waitress for a year, then part-time as a Spanish language teacher. But working odd jobs and being utterly unable to find a job even remotely connected to her fields of expertise, while seeing friends gainfully employed in their fields and people around her easily getting full time work, were almost as painful as being totally unemployed.

She was in a bind. Her qualification as a psychologist in Spain could not be recognized in Australia until she completed a two-year Master's Degree in Psychology from a local university or

Technique Seven: Calling S.O.S. to the Universe

was accepted into an internship program of similar duration. Either way, she needed to take an English language test and get extremely high scores.

There are times we desperately need to get something and we are told we have to do this or do that so we can get what we want. We react and try to do everything that we are told to do, only to find that in the end we can't get what we want after all.

Nadia applied to psychology programs in a couple of universities but was immediately rejected; places were very limited and competition was extremely fierce, she was told. She took an English language test, needing to score at least an 8 over-all. She scored a dismal 5. There was no hope for her to ever reach the required score, not unless there was a computer somewhere that she could plug her brain to, à la Neo in the Matrix, which would instantly upload the entire English language into her brain, and make her cry "Whoa, I know English!" So, she gave up trying to be a psychologist in Australia.

She was told several times during interviews that she was not hired because she didn't have local knowledge and experience. Having given up on psychology, she did the next best thing, which was to go back to school to study counselling. She took on a sizeable student loan, and trudged through almost 2 years of graduate school. She gained some local experience when she did a voluntary and unpaid internship at a small hospital that specialized in mental health. She completed her degree and was awarded accreditation at the highest counselling level. She continued applying for jobs, but this time in counselling. After all that she had done and been through, she believed that surely her dream job would now come quickly. She was wrong.

Then there was the matter of money. From her job as a waitress and her intermittent work as a Spanish language teacher, she never earned more than $5,000 in a year. She survived only through the financial support of her parents.

She continued applying for jobs, writing long applications and sending her resumes. The rejections kept coming. It seemed clear, after all those rejections, that the job market for counsellors seemed pretty closed to her. No one seemed interested in the least to hire a bilingual Spanish-English speaking, newly-graduated counsellor, who possessed zero paid counselling experience in Australia.

For Nadia, being unable to find work in her field for years was like entering a dark tunnel. She entered it as soon as she arrived in Australia; she did not enter by her own choice and she was unaware of just how dark or long the tunnel was. She entered, hoping that the tunnel wouldn't be that dark, and believing that surely there would be sporadic rays of light to illuminate her path. She walked in, optimistic that while it may be dark, the tunnel wouldn't be that long. Surely it would not take her long to reach the other side?

Then the tunnel grew darker and darker still; she kept walking yet the tunnel seemed to stretch endlessly. Many times, she felt like she was walking in circles or going backwards even. Days turned into weeks, weeks lengthened into months, and months stretched into years.

In early 2018, Nadia had almost reached breaking point. She left Spain for Australia in search of a better, happier, more secure future. But after five years of fruitless job-searching, her prospects looked so bleak that she often wondered whether it was best to just pack everything up and go back to Spain.

Writing to the Universe

I taught Nadia this powerful writing technique after I had used it myself with amazing results. She had always been skeptical of anything that sounded supernatural or spiritual. Yet she was left with very few choices. She was willing to try anything, desperate to put her faith in something.

Technique Seven: Calling S.O.S. to the Universe

In April 2018, after yet another job rejection, Nadia wrote a hand-written letter, on yellow legal pad, addressed to the Universe. Nothing in her experience told her or even suggested to her that doing something as crazy as writing a letter to an unseen entity or force would work. And yet, she wrote.

"Dear Universe…"

In a two-and-a-half page letter, written in plain, simple English, she described the problem to the Universe, adding exactly how she felt at that moment. She wrote from her heart and did not sugar-coat anything. Apart from my minor grammatical corrections, I have quoted the following passages from her letter verbatim.

> *I am really worried about my situation that is at 37 years old I still don't have a fulfilled job as a counsellor/ psychologist. I left my family and friends 5 years ago because I wanted to find my way, a job that would give me money, satisfactions, success. I feel stressed, frustrated because of this and because I want to be able to use my skills, education and years of sacrifice like all.*

She did not try to be cheerful or positive; instead, she wrote down all her fears on paper. She left nothing unwritten.

> *I am worried because I don't have money in my account and every time I look at it I feel bad because it's empty. I am scared that if one day I need money for any emergency that comes out I can't pay for it. I am frustrated because I want to contribute more with the home expenses (ex. rent, food, bills, home loan). I feel sad because I can't send money to support my mother that now she is alone…I am*

> *afraid of my lack of money/job, this makes me nervous and stressed and I don't want to be like this.*

Then she told the Universe exactly what she wanted. As she did when she listed down her fears, this time, she did not hold back. She stated exactly what she wanted and asked the Universe to give it.

> *I want to work in a medical center beside other professionals like me that gives me a salary of $80,000 per year. Where I am appreciated by my co-workers, my boss, colleagues and clients. Where I can bring out all my skills, qualifications and experiences.*

It's interesting that she wrote such a specific figure as her desired annual salary. The fact that this figure was 27 times more than what she ever earned working in any job in Australia was not lost on her. Yet, this is what she wanted and it was what she asked for.

She described in detail the kind of working environment she wanted to be in, injecting as much honest feelings in her words as she could.

> *A place where I can work and be loved by every one, I can be distinguished, recognized and well-known in Sydney and Australia.*

She included even the little things in her request.

> *I want to have a bonus laptop, my personal room with my name near the door, saying 'Counsellor and Psychotherapist'.*

After writing her short letter, she thanked the Universe and described how she now felt after writing. She also wrote as if the things she had asked for were now hers.

> *Thank you so much for fulfilling my desire. Thank you Universe for this wonderful job that you gave to me. My partner, my mother, my dad and family are all proud of me. I feel better now looking at my account increasing every two weeks because of my income. I feel relieved now. I can finally contribute with the expenses to the family and buy anything I want without thinking twice before I do it. Thank you Universe for my success and fulfillment and satisfactions. I really appreciate it that you listened to my words and prayer. I feel light and relieved.*

She folded the letter, put it in an envelope, sealed it and wrote "To the Universe" outside it. She put in a special box and tucked it away in a corner of the top shelf of her wardrobe. She did her best to forget about the letter, and in time, she eventually forgot that it was even there.

The Universe responds

In the next few months after she wrote the letter, Nadia stopped applying for jobs all together. Not because she had given up looking for her job, but she had reached the point where she knew that doing more of what she had already been doing in the last few years would not help. Instead, she totally removed her focus from her unemployment and busied herself with other things and pursuing other activities she really enjoyed doing, like knitting and doing yoga. She also continued doing her best in the other casual jobs that came her way.

At first nothing happened. Nothing seemed to happen. Then things began developing, slowly at first, but quickly progressing in a way that she never could have expected. In October, she received a call from a recruiter about a role that he thought Nadia would be perfect for. The recruiter sounded genuinely enthusiastic, something that was uncommon in Nadia's experience. His client, a non-profit organization that served the Spanish-Australian community in Sydney, was looking for a Gambling Help Support Officer. The role required a registered counsellor with experience in counselling people dealing with gambling and other addictions, and who was fluent in Spanish and English.

He said, going quickly to the point, that Nadia would be perfect for the role.

Right after the call, Nadia realized that she had already applied for a job to this organization and interviewed with them several years ago. At that time, they were looking for an Australian psychologist, which she was not. When she interviewed with them originally, they were looking for someone fluent in both English and Spanish and her English level was not good back then. She doubted whether things had changed enough that she would be successful this time in getting into the same organization that had rejected her four years ago. She remembered her letter to the Universe and decided to give it one more shot.

From there, things escalated. A series of interviews followed, including the ultimate interview with the general manager of the organization, the human resources manager and resident psychologist. Nadia received a lot of support from the recruiter himself, who coached her on the possible questions she might get asked, as well as another friend who had also worked for that organization as a counsellor. During her last interview with the organization four years ago, she lacked confidence, and was nervous and anxious. This was picked up by the interviewers right away. This

Technique Seven: Calling S.O.S. to the Universe

time, after years of preparation and waiting for this time to come, she carried an easy confidence and assurance, which was palpable throughout her interview. The interviewers congratulated her on how well she spoke English.

Almost one week after the interview, the recruiter called her to give her the good news that she was successful in getting the job. Nadia received her contract by email and post a few days later. When she read the contract, she happily confirmed that practically all of the things she had asked from the Universe in her letter – from the duties required, the working conditions, and the benefits – had been granted. The organization would pay for her to buy a car or a laptop. And the salary?

It was $81,000 per year.

Try it yourself: Letter to the Universe technique

Here are the steps. Choose a time and place where you can write uninterrupted for as long as you need to finish writing the letter. Take a plain sheet of paper and with pen in hand, just simply write.

One: "Dear Universe…"

As you write these words, suspend any feelings of disbelief or doubt you might have as to whether this will work or not. Believe even for a moment that someone, something possessed of infinite wisdom, knowledge and power is reading your words as you write them. More importantly, trust for a moment that this someone or something you are writing to also loves and cares for you to an immeasurable degree. Let this knowledge sink in, allow yourself to be assured and be humbled by it.

Two: "Here's my problem / situation…"

Imagine that the Universe, the source of all there ever was, is and will be, who sees and knows all things, is now listening to you state your problem. And know that there is absolutely nothing you can write or say that will be a surprise to the Universe. Whatever your problem is, it is nothing new to the Universe, which has heard and seen it all before.

Three: "I am afraid that…"

State to the Universe what it is that you fear about your situation. Explain your worries, doubts and concerns, and all that is making you anxious and stressed out about your problem. Don't hold back – if you want to describe the worst-case scenario (even if your rational mind tells you that it is not likely to happen), then do so.

Imagine, too, that while you are stating your fears to the Universe, stating your case as it were, that it listens to you with infinite patience, and completely without judgment. You could tell the Universe that you're worried your entire world will crumble and fall and it would be unfazed. Even if, on the face of it, your situation does seem hopeless or you were partly or wholly responsible for you being in this mess, say this and be completely confident that you will not be judged for what you have written. Give yourself complete permission to wallow in negativity, because guess what? The Universe gives you permission.

Even if you can't imagine the magnitude of the thought that the Universe is listening to you state your fears, simply doing this step helps you put your fears into perspective. As you take your fears out of your mind, where they are prone to all sorts of suggestions and musings that could aggravate them, and write them out on paper, you put them into perspective. And most of the time,

Technique Seven: Calling S.O.S. to the Universe

you immediately see that some of your fears are unfounded and exaggerated.

Four: "Here's what I want…"

Now that you have wallowed in negativity, laid out all that could possibly go wrong with your situation, and spelled out all that you do not want to happen, tell the Universe exactly what you want. Describe everything that you want to have or happen in the minutest detail. Again, as with step three, know that whatever you might tell the Universe about what you want, the Universe has heard it all before. There is absolutely nothing you can ask for that is a surprise to the Universe; but more important, there is nothing that you could ask that the Universe cannot provide. Be confident that there is no outcome so fantastic or a result so wonderful as to be beyond the Universe's ability to create.

As God once asked Abraham, "Is anything too wonderful for the Lord?" We know that the answer to this question is a resounding "no!". So, we should take it on faith that there really is nothing too wonderful or impossible for God to achieve if we can only believe.

Allow yourself to be totally unrealistic in this step. Even if you hear a voice in your head tell you, "yeah right, that will never happen!" or "you wish!" silence it and keep on writing. Remember, what you want is between you and the Universe, it is no one else's business.

Five: "Thank you for coming through for me."

Gratitude is one of the most powerful forces in all of creation. When you give thanks to the Universe for already fixing your issue or solving your problem for you, even when you see no evidence of it, your faith becomes unshakeable. In this step, it is not uncommon for people to be filled with a sense of "peace that goes beyond all understanding". In this step, you may also want to describe to the Universe the immense sense of relief that you now feel and thank it for handling this matter for you so completely and wonderfully.

Six: "Now I let it go, become still and wait."

Sign your letter, put it in an envelope and seal it, or place it in a special box that you will now tuck away hidden from view. You have done everything you need to and can do. There is nothing else to be done. Again, allow yourself to be filled with immense relief and even joyous expectation knowing that a power beyond anything you could ever comprehend or imagine is now at work to orchestrate the most perfect and complete solution to your problem.

Be still, knowing that help is on its way and that it will not be a second late. Find assurance in the knowledge that when the solution to your problem comes, it will come in a way or a form that you could never have devised or created through your own power or ability.

Key points to remember

In step 3, don't worry about being too negative or that by writing your worst fears on paper, you are focusing on the negative and so might attract more negative outcomes. Your fears are your fears and no one has the right to say that your fears are silly or unfounded. Whatever you write down as your fears and worries is a matter between you and the Universe.

For step 4, start by simply listing down the things you want or would like to happen. To make this more powerful, describe what you really want. Take the things you wrote in your list and elevate them – use active, descriptive words like "I am enjoying this," or "I am so excited that". Write until you start feeling that what you want is actually present and on its way to you. Keep writing until

Technique Seven: Calling S.O.S. to the Universe

you start feeling good about your situation. Then ramp everything up even more. Write as if you already possess the things you want or what you would like to happen already has and now you're looking back from your current position to the time when you wrote your letter.

For step 6, as with what Nadia did, while you are waiting for the Universe to answer, do your best not to be anxious. Keep yourself busy with other things you enjoy doing. In the same way that Nadia stopped applying for jobs entirely during the period she waited, you might even want to stop doing anything that is an attempt to fix your problem. Remember, you have already assigned this job to the Universe and it can do it infinitely better than you can. Relax and enjoy the process of waiting.

Technique Eight: Vision Mapping

Set a course to your true life vision

"Imagine the grandest possible vision of your life, for you become what you believe."

—Oprah Winfrey

I am in my study at home as I write the opening words of this chapter. I look to my right at one of my vision boards (I have a couple hanging up on my study walls). This particular vision board is divided into two sections. The top section contains images of things that are yet to become. The bottom section contains photos of past significant successes and achievements. These latter images remind me that at many points in my life, I have successfully achieved goals that were once impossible to me when they were set.

One of the photos shows a bridge over a river at sunset. Most people will look at this photo and think that this is just a generic photo of a sunset water vista. But those closest to me will know that it is a photo of a vision realized.

It was 2005. I was working as a lawyer in a prestigious law firm in Manila. While my job had all the trappings of success, and represented a place, position, and status that I had once only dreamed of, I could not deny that my days working in a corporate law firm were numbered. I had not yet told my family, but I also knew that my days living in my birth country, close to them, were also numbered.

I knew that I was being called (pulled?) to go out into the world. At that point, I did not know precisely where, but soon an unshakeable sense that I was meant to come to Australia overcame me. This made no sense at the time – I did not know anyone in Australia, I knew no Australians (apart from an old girlfriend I met in Manila but whom I was no longer in communication with), and I did not know anything about the country apart from what I had learned from a five-day visit there two years prior.

The feeling that I had to go to and be in Australia was so overwhelming that I had to capture it somehow to make sense out of it. To keep the vision in front of me as often as possible, I looked for a photo that represented Australia. I found photos of random Australian scenes in a back issue of Reader's Digest, on a page announcing some sort of travel deal to Australia. I did not know exactly which parts of the country these photos depicted and I did not care. These photos were in a travel ad for Australia and that was good enough for me

I cut out one photo, which was about the size of a matchbox, and taped it onto the top of my computer monitor at work. The photo showed an image of a nameless bridge over a nameless river at sunset, supposedly somewhere in Australia. I would stare at that photo every day at work for more than a year.

In the ensuing months, I made tentative plans to come to Australia. Nothing concrete, certainly nothing definite enough to justify telling the partners at my law firm that I needed to go on indefinite leave. But by the start of 2006, I had made the decision that I was going to Australia one way or another. In May that year, I wrote down the following in my Think and Decree notebook:

Technique Eight: Vision Mapping

I want to work, live, build and establish ties in Australia. I want to experience life there for an extended period of time (at least 5 years) and I want this to happen by January 2007.

I had never done something like this before – simply packing up, leaving my beloved family, my lucrative lawyer job, and the only country I had ever known, and moving to a completely foreign land. I knew it was illogical, irrational, perhaps mad. And yet once I had written down my vision on paper, I was confident it was inevitable that it would eventually come to pass.

A mere five months after writing down that statement, and more than a year after I cut out that photo of bridge at sunset over a nameless river in Australia, I landed in Melbourne. I arrived in the morning, checked into my hostel and promptly passed out for the next several hours.

When I woke up, I saw that I had slept for almost seven hours. I was famished, not having eaten anything since the flight. I had never been to Melbourne before, and did not know where to go to eat. So, I thought of stepping out of my hostel and walking as far as I could until I found a restaurant.

I started walking, with not a restaurant or shopping mall in sight. The sun was starting to set as I crossed a bridge over a river. My Lonely Planet map told me that this was the Yarra River, famous in Australia. As I reached the middle of the bridge, despite my hunger, something made me stop and turn to look at the sunset.

It was in profound awe that I realized that I was looking at the exact same image that was in the photo pasted on my computer monitor. My vision had become my vivid, living reality.

Visionaries or 'woonatics'?

I was at a seminar attended by some pretty smart people – PHDs, lawyers, accountants – and I was sitting beside a man. He had been a partner at a global accounting firm for many years and was now a lecturer at a small business school in Sydney. He seemed, by most standards, a reasonably successful man. But I sensed that something was missing from this person. He seemed bored. Too bored in fact.

The topic that came up for discussion was success advice. Each participant was asked, "what advice would you give to your 20-year-old self if you could?" Someone, somewhere in the room mouthed the word vision; the word was said just loud enough and it floated around until it reached the ears of the man sitting beside me. His ears picked up at the sound of the word 'vision'. He scoffed and said, it seemed more to himself than to me, 'I'd tell my younger self that vision is just a load of crap, a bunch of woo-woo if you ask me."

At that instant, I knew what it was that I had sensed the first time I spoke with him. He seemed lifeless and it was because, at that moment in his life, he had already lost the capacity to possess and be driven by a vision. He no longer had the passion to envision something worth going after in his life. Perhaps once when he was 20 years old he had a vision. But a lifetime of going against the true calling of his vision had dulled his mind to it.

"Cherish your visions and dreams, as they are the children of your soul, the blueprints of your ultimate destiny." Napoleon Hill, one of the most influential writers of the 20th century and one of the fathers of the self-help movement, said that. Study history and you will find that the people who did cherish their visions are the ones who have achieved the highest standards in their chosen fields and left lasting legacies. It appears to be a rule of life that people who hear the call of their true visions and have the courage to follow

Technique Eight: Vision Mapping

it are the ones who achieve the most success. I'm ticking off people in my head as they come and I find that there is no exception to it.

Imagine if Jeff Bezos stayed as an employee on Wall Street – Amazon.com would never have been created. What if Tiger Woods didn't think he was good enough to keep working at being a pro golfer? What if Michael Jordan believed the high school coach who cut him from the varsity team because he (Jordan) wasn't a good enough basketball player? Then the 20th century would have been denied two of the world's greatest sports icons.

What if Oprah Winfrey did not listen to the still voice in her 25-year-old self that a black woman from America's deep south, someone born into poverty, someone who most of the world would not call physically beautiful, could become one of the most successful television personalities and later media moguls in America? Then she would have grown up mired in the same poverty and mediocrity that generations of her family before her had grown up in. What if Tony Robbins did not listen to the call in his heart to start helping people find passion in life even though he did not have any sort of degree in psychology? Then the world would have lost one of its most influential teachers of human potential.

People say that someone successful was born to do whatever it was that made them successful. Mozart was born to compose great music. Einstein was born to be a great scientist. Bill Gates was born to be an entrepreneur. I don't buy that. I don't believe that anyone is necessarily born to be something. What I do believe is that each of us is born with a unique set of special gifts.

At one point or various points in our lives, something strikes us that we can be something or do something special in this life, something that makes our hearts pound with excitement and keeps us awake at nights. We might see someone doing something and we say to ourselves, "that's what I want to do!" Or we might initially sense that we are being pulled to do something, even though it is the craziest, most irrational thing. These are our visions being born inside of us. I believe each of us has a choice right then and there whether or not to take steps to pursue that vision.

It is possible that vision is not required to achieve worldly success; but I do know that it is indispensable to happiness, satisfaction and fulfillment in life. And most often, success is a by-product of happiness, satisfaction and fulfilment. The interesting thing about vision is that those who pursue it, not because they want to be rich and famous, but because it is something they just have to do in order for them to be happy and fulfilled in life, are the ones who end up rich, famous and successful anyway.

Hamburgers and French fries on parade

In 1954, a 52-year-old Czech-born American milkshake mixer salesman, found himself stupefied. Sales of his company's multi-mixers had plummeted due to competition from a rival company's lower-priced products. But a small restaurant in San Bernardino, California had just bought eight of his multi-mixers. "What kind of outfit would need eight of these things?" the salesman wondered to himself.

At that age, most people would probably have entertained their curiosity with as much attention as changing TV channels. Most people his age would probably not have bothered checking out this restaurant, thinking they can't be bothered because they are about 13 years from retirement. This salesman though was different. His curiosity was piqued and he visited the restaurant.

In his line of work, he had seen perhaps a thousand restaurant kitchens. It took him just one look at that small restaurant, which by then only had three outlets, to know that there was something bigger, much bigger in store for it.

Technique Eight: Vision Mapping

"When I saw it working that day in 1954, I felt like some latter-day Newton who'd just had an Idaho potato caromed off his skull," the salesman would later write. That night in his motel room, he did a lot of heavy thinking about what he'd seen during the day. He was convinced that the concept and design of this tiny restaurant chain had the potential to grow across the country. In his own words, visions of these restaurants "dotting crossroads all over the country paraded through my brain".

That salesman was Ray Kroc and that restaurant was McDonalds. The vision that struck him on that fateful fay in 1954 was so forceful that it would drive him for the rest of his life. Such is the power of a compelling vision. Ray Kroc envisioned his restaurant empire long before it was material fact. He envisioned the path to get to that image in his mind. His vision would later be embodied in the McDonald's motto of "Quality, service, cleanliness and value" and he spent the rest of his life convincing thousands of employees to share in that vision.

Powerful as his vision was, however, I doubt even he knew exactly just how powerful and all-encompassing it would be once it was unleashed. As of 2020, according to Investopedia.com, McDonald's has more than 38,600 outlets in over 100 countries.

Feeling the vision

The dictionary definition of "vision" is "a mental image of what the future will or could be like". It also means "the faculty of being able to see" or "the ability to think about or plan the future with imagination or wisdom".

These definitions lead me to ask, what if you are unable to see a mental image of the future? What if you are not a "visually-oriented" person? What if you can't imagine the future? Does that mean you can't have a vision?

The concept that vision should involve the ability to vividly see the future in all its minutest details discourages many people who, for one reason or another, find it hard to imagine pictures and images in their head. But you don't need to be able to see what the future will or could be like to have vision. You could also *feel* what the future will or could be like.

This is why I prefer to use the word "envision" when teaching techniques relating to creating a vision. To "envision" means "to imagine as a future possibility". But we don't only imagine by seeing things; we imagine by feeling things as well.

The normal route to visualization is to think of a picture in your mind and to hold on to that image until it produces feelings. It's the feelings that contain the good stuff; feelings are the things that move us to act on the external world. Ancient eastern spiritual traditions have taught that our feelings can and do actually shape external reality. Images by themselves are not creative; it is images fuelled by feelings that are creative.

Jonathan Swift said that vision "is the art of seeing the invisible". But I am going to revise that quote by saying that vision "is the art of *feeling* the invisible". You can envision things by first feeling the feelings you believe you will experience were you to achieve your goal or desire.

In my own experience, it has often been the feeling of what my future will or could be like if I pursue a certain goal that has impelled me to take massive action. I find it hard to sit in a chair for an extended period of time and mentally imagine the details of what I want to happen. Visualization is like meditation – it's hard to keep your mind focused on what you're doing; stray thoughts begin to intrude the moment you start it. Instead, I find it so much easier to start by feeling what I would feel if my goal were achieved. And when I start envisioning by first feeling things, I find that the mental images naturally come. Remember this thought, emblazon it in your mind and repeat it as a mantra daily:

Emotion Empowers your Envisioning

Infusing life into your vision: Vision Mapping

African American New Thought Minister and Author Michael Beckwith said that "pain pushes until vision pulls." A vision must be compelling otherwise it won't pull you.

Ari Weinzweig, founding partner of Zingerman's, which Inc. magazine called "the coolest small company in America" explained that an effective vision needs to be:

- Inspiring: it has to inspire all who will be involved in implementing it.

- Strategically sound: you must actually have a decent shot at making it happen.

- Documented: it must be written down to make it work.

- Communicated: you actually have to tell people about it

How Vision Mapping Works

A vision consistently held in one's mind for an extended period of time is powerful. But what's exceedingly and immensely more powerful is a vision that has been taken from one's mind and put in tangible form.

We've heard of the expression "out of sight, out of mind". If something is only inside your head, then you risk forgetting that vision. You could be distracted by other visions. If you keep an image locked away in your mind, there is a danger that that image will be diluted with the passing of time.

"Front of sight, front of mind" is what I would say. I would also say: "In sight, in mind, inspired in progress." When you take that vision in your head and write it down on paper, you liberate it. Throughout this book, I've frequently described writing as a unique psychoneuromotor activity, which means that when you write something, at that moment, your mind and body are united in a single act; and at that moment, your actions create all-powerful feelings. When you write your vision down on paper, and you begin to describe the details of your goal or dream, you stir up feelings that fuel your vision. Later on, after you've finished writing your vision, you can re-read it and as you do so, you again generate these all-powerful feelings that stoke the fire of your vision.

Vision Mapping works because it frees your mind from the material sense of quantity and quality and reminds you that creation starts in the mind and continues outward in the physical realm.

Another huge reason why Vision Mapping works is because when you write down or "map" your vision on paper, you can more easily share it with others. If your vision requires many people to "buy in" to what you want to happen, if it involves their cooperation and coordinated effort, then you need to be able to describe it to them in detail. Unless you plan to individually describe your vision to each and every person who's required to hear it, you should write it down and share it with them. They can read your vision repeatedly and be inspired by it.

Never underestimate the power of a compelling vision that has been written down and described on paper. Some of the most famous political and religious ideologies were propagated by means of a founder writing down his or her original vision and having proponents of that vision pass on what was written to others. And if your vision is compelling enough, then your associates will want to

Technique Eight: Vision Mapping

share your vision to others and inspire them as well. It's possible to do this when your vision has been written down on paper.

Try it yourself: Vision Mapping

I created Vision Mapping and it's a hybrid of different other writing techniques I've learned and practiced through the years – including those techniques described in *Chapter 3 Life Scripting* – as well as other techniques like Ari Weinzweig's visioning process. Feel free to adopt aspects of what is useful from the technique described below with other similar techniques you've discovered or are using. Take a cue from Bruce Lee who said, "adapt what is useful, reject what is useless, and add what is specifically your own." There is no 100 percent correct way to do Vision Mapping. As with any of the techniques I've taught in this book, the important thing is that you actually start writing.

Step 1. Choose the area to envision

One knock on the word "vision" is that it only deals with big, grand things. Having a "life vision" intimidates and turns off many people because for so many of us, we don't even know what we will be doing in 12 or 6 months' time, let alone the rest of our lives!

I totally agree with Ari Weinzweig when he explained that you can set a vision for all size projects and to suit every budget. If, like me, you're a "big picture" person, then by all means write out a big, grand life vision. I wrote one and named it *"Master Lifeplan 2026"*. You can download a template from www.WriteTech.co/resources. But you can envision something happening in 6 to 12 months, like your perfect wedding, a 7-country trip, or your house renovation, or for an even longer period, like bigger changes you want in your business 5 years from now.

Step 2. Decide the timeline

In the case of the Zingerman organization, Weinzweig explains that they set anything from two to 10-year visions, with 5 years being the typical period. But if you're new to envisioning, you can also start with a smaller one to 6-month project.

Step 3. Identify the milestones

Milestones will represent what success will look like to you as you go through the process of living out your vision. Big successes almost often comprise several, smaller, but significant, successes. Think about the ultimate result you want to achieve. What are the milestones that would have to be reached to build up to the big victorious result? Don't take too much time listing them – Weinzweig typically spends 10 minutes. You can always add more later on.

The idea is to get you to see that even extraordinary, remarkable results seem more achievable when broken down into milestones. And while we can be excited when imagining the big results, often, it's the smaller, but no less significant milestones on the way to the summit, which can really pump us and keep us pushing forward.

Step 4. Write out your vision

Write out the first draft of your vision. Adopting Weinzweig's example for Zingerman's, you might start out by writing: "It's (put down the timeline you've decided on above). There are so many great things happening that make it clear that our long-term vision has become the reality that we hoped and believed it would back when we wrote it."

Don't dwell too long on this step. Half an hour is a good amount of time to spend on it. Just keep writing until your time

Technique Eight: Vision Mapping

is up. Then forget about the draft for a few days or even longer as required by your project.

The fact that it's a first draft is important both practically and symbolically. Practically, it reminds you that this only a first attempt; it doesn't have to be perfect. Far from it! You're only after the minimum result at this time. You'll do several drafts later on don't worry.

Symbolically, it reminds you that a vision is a dynamic representation of what you would like things to be. It's something that's evolving, not static or set in stone.

There are no set rules on how to write your vision. Remember that your vision is unique to you. I highly encourage you, though, to envision something grand. Refer back to what Oprah Winfrey said at the start of this chapter. A vision is meant to pull you with such force that you almost have no choice but to pursue it. And to do that, your vision must be big. At the same time, you must be honest with your vision. Write from your core. Don't go for something big or grand (I see myself listing my company on the New York Stock Exchange!) just because that's what success looks like in your chosen field or area of endeavor. This is your personal vision, so it should excite you and make you believe in the unlimited possibilities waiting for you. But above all, your vision should fill you (not other people) with joy and peace.

Write that vision in white heat. Read about this technique in *Chapter 6 Super Conscious Writing*. Write fast and resist the temptation to edit, critique or criticize yourself or what you are writing. Get the whole vision out from your brain onto paper, even if the initial product may be rough on the edges. That's ok. Writing the first draft is like running a sprint – your aim is to start fast and complete it quickly. I recommend no more than 15 minutes for this.

Step 5. Revise your vision

Read your first draft in its entirety. A first draft will never be perfect – it's not meant to be. But what it should be – and what your vision should always be – is inspiring. Reading that first draft should make you more excited (even slightly nervous which is a good thing) as you read it. Pay close attention to what you wrote in that first draft. If you wrote honestly and from your core, then it will likely contain the seed, the kernel of your vision. As such, it's the expression of your vision at its most authentic.

This doesn't mean that you can't improve on the original expression of your vision. For the succeeding drafts, aim for specificity. Be very specific and write in as many fine details as possible when revising your draft. Feel free to do further drafts if you feel like you have to, but a maximum of four redrafts is best.

Step 6. Get trusted feedback

This includes getting feedback from other decision-makers if you're not the only one and you're writing out an organizational vision. It's important that they are sold on your vision because it affects them too. Unless you are all agreed on the vision of what you want your organization or company to be or where you want it to go, you can't move forward. Weinzweig shared the technique they use: they set a topic and time line for the vision, and then have each of the directors or partners write their own vision (no peeking at others' visions!). Once done, everyone compares their drafts, combines common themes and proceeds from there.

You also ask for feedback on your draft from those trusted others whose opinion you respect and value, but who are not necessarily insiders to the organization. As it is your vision, it's possible that you're too close to it and tend to be blind to its flaws. Use outsiders' feedback to improve, not water down, your vision. If anyone tells you that your vision is not doable or realistic, hear

Technique Eight: Vision Mapping

what they have to say, but remember that you don't have to listen to them.

Step 7. Get hustling!

Now it's time to share your vision on a wholescale level – that is, with all those who will take part in executing it or will be affected by it. It's true, as Weinzweig says, that starting out with a grand vision doesn't mean that you will achieve it 100 percent, in the same way that not writing out your vision doesn't mean you'll fail. But (and this is one of the most important principles that permeate this entire book) desiring something and writing it down on paper gives it life. As it says in Proverbs 29:18: "where there is no vision, the people perish". If you have no written vision of your organization's future, then you cannot share it widely, and unless you do this, your team cannot move together toward an exciting, challenging and empowering version of that future.

Key points to remember

Don't hold back when envisioning. Here's something that I've personally found useful to do: think that you're the founder and CEO of your own hugely successful company and this vision will be emailed to the 1,000 people (or 5,000, or 10,000) in your organization who helped bring it to where it is today. Envisioning is all about daring to think as big as you can; so, while you're at it, then think up the biggest possible vision you can find in your heart to think of.

Finally, remember – "front of sight, front of mind". Keep your written vision constantly in front of you; keep it beside you when you sleep, so that it's the last thing you see before you sleep and the first thing you see when you wake up. Watch the awesome miracle of co-creation happen once you release your vision and give it life by constantly giving it your focus and attention.

Technique Nine: Think, Write, Decree

The combustible power of decrees

There are some words that people almost never use in ordinary, daily conversation, at least not if they don't want others to look at them strangely, like they have just said something crazy. And there are also other words that people would never say or imagine themselves as saying, especially after the word "I".

One of these words is "decree". Another of these words is "declare". We never actually say these words anymore, and certainly we never say "I decree this" or "I declare that." You could, but expect the other person to retort, "who made you king or queen?" or "yes your majesty, yes your highness".

This is because a 'decree', as a noun, is an official order that has the force of law, an official statement or order that something must happen. As a verb, a 'decree' means to command something to be done or to happen. A 'declaration' is something similar. It is a formal statement or announcement, written and spoken to tell yourself, others and the world, about something important. To 'declare' something is to say something in a solemn and emphatic manner.

Given the meanings of these words, it's no surprise no one says these words anymore! "I decree that I will go and eat a salad!" "I declare that I go to sleep and wake up at five o'clock a.m.!" These statements are downright silly and use the words "decree" and "declare" in a cavalier, disrespectful manner, without awareness of their true power.

If you say, however, "I decree that I will be successful or rich or healthy" when you've been mediocre or broke or sick all your life and when everyone around you, your whole family and all your friends, have been the same way for as long as you've known them, then the statement takes on significantly more gravity. Suddenly, you're using the word "decree" properly. If you say, "I declare that I am going to quit smoking, eat healthy and run one mile at five o'clock in the morning three times as week", or something so deceptively simple as "I declare that one day I am going to buy that house of my dreams and live in it", or "my business will be a multi-million dollar company in one year's time", or "my children will grow up in the right way" (whatever that means to you), then, you know that whatever you said will happen, it will come to pass.

When you decree or declare something, and really mean it, and use these words the way I will teach you in this chapter, then you will see that things will start to happen in your world. People will start taking notice of you and listening to you. And what you decreed or declared will start to come to pass.

How to slay giants

If you are unconvinced that words, particularly declarations, possess great power, if you think I am deluded for suggesting that declaring something is enough to make things happen, then I invite you to consider the three following declarations.

Technique Nine: Think, Write, Decree

This first declaration was made by a young shepherd boy when faced with the impossible task of slaying a giant.

> *You come against me with sword and spear and javelin, but I come against you in the name of the LORD Almighty, the God of the armies of Israel, whom you have defied.*
>
> *This day the LORD will hand you over to me, and I'll strike you down and cut off your head. Today I will give the carcasses of the Philistine army to the birds of the air and the beasts of the earth, and the whole world will know that there is a God in Israel.*
>
> *All those gathered here will know that it is not by sword or spear that the LORD saves; for the battle is the LORD's, and he will give all of you into our hands.*

Consider this next declaration. It was made by the leaders of thirteen colonies that sought independence from an imperialist empire:

> *When in the course of human events, it becomes necessary for one people to dissolve the political bands which have connected them with another, and to assume among the powers of the earth, the separate and equal station to which the Laws of Nature and of Nature's God entitle them, a decent respect to the opinions of mankind requires that they should declare the causes which impel them to the separation.*
>
> *We hold these truths to be self-evident, that all men are created equal, that they are endowed by their Creator with certain unalienable rights, that among these are Life, Liberty and the pursuit of Happiness.*

That to secure these rights, governments are instituted among Men, deriving their just powers from the consent of the governed, that whenever any form of government becomes destructive of these ends, it is the right of the People to alter or to abolish it.

Finally, consider this last declaration that was uttered by a citizen of a supposedly free nation, when he called on that same nation to fulfill the promise to make all people equal:

Go back to Mississippi, go back to Alabama, go back to South Carolina, go back to Georgia, go back to Louisiana, go back to the slums and ghettos of our northern cities, knowing that somehow this situation can and will be changed. Let us not wallow in the valley of despair.

I say to you today, my friends, so even though we face the difficulties of today and tomorrow, I still have a dream. It is a dream deeply rooted in the American dream.

I have a dream that one day this nation will rise up and live out the true meaning of its creed: "We hold these truths to be self-evident; that all men are created equal."

I have a dream that one day on the red hills of Georgia the sons of former slaves and the sons of former slave owners will be able to sit down together at the table of brotherhood.

I have a dream that one day even the state of Mississippi, a state sweltering with the heat of injustice, sweltering with the heat of oppression, will be transformed into an oasis of freedom and justice.

I have a dream that my four little children will one day live in a nation where they will not be judged by the color of their skin but by the content of their character.

I have a dream today.

Technique Nine: Think, Write, Decree

Consider these three declarations. Consider what they achieved, for the individuals who spoke them, for the people who they spoke the declarations to, and for the people on whose behalf they spoke these declarations.

The first declaration emboldened a young shepherd boy, David, as he faced the giant Goliath in combat. It shored up the young boy's immense inner strength, determination and will to accomplish the seemingly impossible task ahead of him. Most important, it invoked the aid of a higher power to grant him ultimate victory. His declaration inspired his people the Israelites in their struggle against the oppressive Philistines.

The words of the second declaration were unanimously declared on the 4th of July 1776 by the representatives of the 13 united states of America, as they declared their independence from British oppression and sought freedom to chart their own destiny as an independent nation. Similar to what David's words did for him, the words of the United States declaration of independence likewise shored up a people's infinite inner reserves to do what was needed to be done in the face of near impossible odds. In their declaration, they also invoked the aid of divine providence, without which they knew their quest would be futile. Their declaration freed their colonies and led to the founding of what would later become a mighty, free and independent nation.

From the late 1950s to the early 1960s, Martin Luther King Jr frequently invoked Abraham Lincoln's words on equality, themselves drawn from the Declaration of Independence, as he called on the nation to fulfill the quest to make all people equal. Dr King's declaration galvanized an entire country into action, to take steps to bring about the exact dream that he described in his declaration. In time, that dream became real.

Writing declarations down multiplies their power

Here's another key about declarations: writing them down multiplies their power. This is true when you write anything down. I've explained this all throughout the book, from the introduction to the last chapter. I would even go as far as saying that this is the thesis of my book. Writing declarations down harnesses the creative power, which I firmly believe all human beings are endowed with, and kicks this creative power into action. When we declare or decree something, we stamp our imprimatur on those words, and we exercise our God-given power to create and shape reality into whatever form we wish. When we declare or decree something, our energy-harnessing and environment-altering powers are focused in our words; and when these words are declared, they rush to the ends of the universe and come back to us, not empty, but having achieved what we sent them out to achieve.

Why must we write down our declarations? It is because, almost always, people declare to achieve things or bring about outcomes not just for themselves, but also for many others. Writing perpetuates our declarations, and allows them to become immortal. Our creative spirit itself is captured in the very words of our declaration. Our words start to create the moment we speak them. And when others hear our words, then our creative spirit inspires them also; and if they believe what we are declaring, it impels them to unite their own creative impulses with ours, immeasurably increasing the power of our original declaration.

But what happens to those who did not hear our declarations when we spoke them? What about the people who live far away from us or people who have not yet been born and will come into existence long after we are gone? If they do not hear our words, then they will have no chance to capture the essence of what we spoke. Our declarations will not have the chance to inspire them and spur their own creative impulses so that they too take action.

This, simply, is why we must not only speak our declarations, but also write them down: so that others may read them, and in doing so, be galvanized into using their own creative powers to achieve what we originally intended when we first spoke our declarations. We must write our declarations for ourselves too—that we may be constantly reminded of the exact manifestation of reality that we desire our words to achieve.

Decree things to be so, and they will be so. Command things to do what you want, and it will be done for you.

Making a business deal with God

Is it possible to make a business deal with God? Is it even moral to do so? Why is it that in history, whether fictional or actual, we have accounts of people making deals with supernatural forces, anything from gods to the devil, but never with God?

One of the earliest covenants ever made between man and God is recorded in the Bible.

> *And Jacob vowed a vow, saying, If God will be with me, and will keep me in this way that I go, and will give me bread to eat, and raiment to put on, so that I come again to my father's house in peace; then shall the Lord be my God, and this stone, which I have set for a pillar, shall be God's house: and of all that thou shalt give me I will surely give the tenth unto thee. (Genesis 28: 20-22)*

As Catherine Ponder wrote in *The Prosperity Secret of the Ages,* in a business agreement, there is always a party of the first part and a party of the second part. Each party covenants what he or she will do and what he or she expects the other party to do. Jacob covenanted to show his appreciation to God through tithing: "Of all that Thou shalt give me, I will surely give the tenth unto Thee."

I wrote my own covenant with God on January 8, 2010. As of the time of this writing, that was ten years ago. And as I recall that period, I am quietly confident that God has been honoring my covenant with him. This is despite the fact that I have not been perfect – far from it – in honoring my part of the covenant.

You can follow the exact method that Jacob followed: making a definite success covenant with God in which you describe the success you will trust God to help you achieve, and in which you describe what you will do for God in appreciation.

Try it yourself: write your own declarations

Now it's time to write your own declaration. It can be a declaration of accomplishment, in which you specifically state the outcome you wish to obtain in your life.

It can also be a declaration of independence from a certain condition, such as sickness or depression; or state of being, such as mediocrity, misery or unhappiness; or undesirable circumstances, such as financial indebtedness or poverty; or addictions of whatever kind.

It can be a declaration that from this moment forward, no matter what may happen in your future or what life may throw your way, you are declaring that you are free from whatever it is that used to enslave you. Or it can be a declaration that you're simply drawing a line in the sand: that from now on, this is how you are going to live your life, that these are the acts that you will do from now on, or that these are the things that you will not do, accept or put up with.

We will pattern it after some of the most powerful declarations ever made in human history. Throughout the process

Technique Nine: Think, Write, Decree

described below, the words "declare", "declaration" and "decree" are interchangeable.

Step 1: Write the Preamble.

Why are you writing this declaration now? What is it that you want to happen as a result of making this declaration? What do you want to achieve? What do you want to declare independence from? And most important, why do you want to achieve what you want to achieve, why do you want to be free from whatever it is you seek independence from?

Step 2: List down your self-evident truths.

Write down what you hold to be true about you, what you believe and hold sacred, and what you will always hold onto. List down your truths, the beliefs that you now choose to hold, regardless of what may happen around you or what other people say or believe about you, and in the face of all opposition from internal or external forces.

Write down your self-evident truths. Then write down why you choose to hold on to these truths. You might list down the conditions that made it absolutely necessary for you to finally write your own declaration.

Step 3: Explain why you are left with no other recourse.

Explain what will happen to you personally, and the people that you love, if your current condition, state of being, or undesirable circumstance were to persist. Describe what the price will be for you if things did not change. Tell yourself that things in your life have reached such a stage where you are left with no choice but to draw your own line in the sand – that these are the things you will and will not accept, these are the acts you will and will not do from this moment onwards.

Step 4: Now make your declarations.

You can start by saying who you are. You can say your name, "Now, I, Jane or John Smith…". After your name, you might also add a descriptor of who you are or the person who you want to be or believe you are becoming. You can literally write any words here describing who you are or believe you are.

State that you are making this with single-minded, unwavering, unflinching purpose. If you are making your declaration with other people, then state that you are doing this as a single united action: "we, the Smith family gathered together," or "we, John and Jane Smith acting as one and in agreement," or "we, the founders of XYZ company or organization, in congress, assembled".

State in whose name you are doing this act. "Do, in my own name," or "do, in the name of our family, and by authority of each and every member of our family," or "do, in the name of our founders, investors, partners and associates," or "do in the name of God.…"

Then, actually state that you are making a solemn declaration, writing it down on paper and making it known to the whole world. "I or we solemnly publish and declare." If you've ever said the words "I solemnly declare" before and never kept your word or didn't take it seriously, I urge you now to feel the gravity of what you are writing this time.

Now list down your declarations. "I declare that from now on…" or "I declare that…"

Write each declaration as a simple, single statement. Go straight to the point. Make it punchy. Doing all these will make it easier for you to recall your declarations. Even more critical, these will allow you to actually and easily say your declarations out loud. It's advisable to read your declarations as regularly as possible, and I

Technique Nine: Think, Write, Decree

urge you to actually declare your declarations out loud as often and as much as you can.

Step 5: Finally, call on God's protection over your declaration.

"And for the support of my declaration, firmly relying on divine providence," or other similar words. If you don't believe in God, but believe in some other power, then call on that power to protect your declaration. If you're not spiritual in any sense, then don't sweat it – you can call on your own inner strength, will and power to protect your declaration and see it through.

Step 6: Write what you are giving in exchange for making this solemn covenant, this sacred contract.

Make no mistake about what you're doing: you are entering into the most binding contract of all, for it is not with another person. You are entering this contract with yourself. But it's much more than that, you are making a covenant between you and your God. No, it's not a legal contract – you won't have to go to court or pay a fine if you break it. The consequences, however, could be immeasurably graver, more serious and significant if you fail to make good on your declarations.

We live in a universe that is governed by laws. One of these laws is the law of sowing and reaping, of giving and receiving. Any contract or covenant requires consideration otherwise that contract or covenant will be void, meaningless, and powerless to achieve anything. What is that thing that you are pledging and giving which gives substance to your contract or covenant? Write "I pledge my," or "we mutually pledge to each other," then write whatever it is that you are giving in exchange for this declaration. The act of giving something in exchange for what you want to happen is what seals your covenant.

Step 7: Sign your declaration.

I strongly recommend that you write out your declaration by hand, on paper, and sign it with your name and signature, just as you would any legal contract. Or if you have terrible handwriting, or have not held a pen and actually written something on paper in years, then it's also ok to type your declaration and print it out on paper. But you must sign it.

The act of signing, as in any contract or covenant, makes it binding. And when you sign your declaration, you are entering into a solemn, unbreakable covenant with a higher power. It does not matter what you believe that higher power to be, whether it's God, infinite intelligence, Allah, the universe, divine providence or simply your own inner, infinite self. When you sign your declaration, you allow that higher power to achieve exceedingly, abundantly, above and beyond all that you could ever ask or imagine.

Technique Ten: Discernment of the Spirits

A full-proof 400-year-old decision-making technique

I give credit and thanks to my brother, Dennis, for teaching me the essence of the discernment process, which I have adopted and modified into the writing technique described in this chapter.

In 2005, I was at a crossroads in my life. I had already achieved my childhood dream of becoming a lawyer, just like my father and mother before me. I had found a secure and stable job in a prestigious law firm in Manila. My work was interesting, challenging and mentally-stimulating. I worked in a collegial environment. I was also being paid good money and receiving all the perks and bonuses, including yearly all expenses paid trips to Europe, America and other countries, which came with working in a high-powered legal career. I was well on the way to a successful career as a lawyer. The next 30 years of that career stretched out before me like an endless road.

That thought depressed me. I should have been happy with where I was, but I was not. Have you ever had had that experience where everything is going right in your life, in your personal relationships and career, yet you can't shake off the feeling that something is missing, that you were meant to be or do something else and until you find out what that something was, you would never be at peace? This was my exact feeling back then. I could not understand it and it bothered me enough to know that if I didn't do something about it, I would forever carry what would later be explained to me as a "holy dissatisfaction".

I turned to my brother Dennis for guidance. I went to him not just because he was my brother, who knew me better than almost anyone else, but because he had training in discernment. At that time, Dennis was in the seminary where he was studying to be a priest under the tutelage of the Jesuits. The Jesuits were among the first psychoanalysts and counsellors.

For centuries, the Jesuits had been teaching a method to help guide people going through difficult life choices. This method was called the Discernment of the Spirits and was created by Ignatius of Loyola, the founder of the Jesuit order. His discernment technique is a powerful tool for making major, life-altering decisions. In developing this technique, Ignatius was ahead of his time since he combined rational thinking with psychology and spirituality.

Today, Ignatius' Spiritual Exercises, of which the Discernment of the Spirits is part, are being used by thought leaders of all beliefs and persuasions as a powerful decision-making tool. Rick Warren, author of *A Purpose Driven Life* for instance, uses the spiritual exercises to guide his readers. My brother adapted the spiritual exercises and used it to counsel everyone from executives to students to couples and retirees, guiding them to make critical, life-altering decisions. Other authors have realized the power of these spiritual exercises as well.

To 'discern' something is to 'perceive, recognize or find out'. 'Discernment' is the process of perceiving right from wrong, truth from error, making distinctions between them, and carefully choosing between the two. The method that I learned involved discerning several choices open to me and testing them over and over through the course of several months. Throughout the whole process, I was taught that it was essential that I wrote down everything that was going on in my mind, as well as the outcomes I was seeing manifested in my external world.

Testing the Spirits

Why did I feel the need to consult an advisor like my brother when I was facing a decision to leave my family, country and career behind and move to another country? Why couldn't I make this decision in the same way I make other decisions? After all, whether big or small, it's a decision, right?

I didn't see it that way. I knew that the decision facing me was momentous. I was absolutely convinced that whichever way I chose would determine the rest of my life. I needed a way to make a decision anchored on wisdom and prudence, not on emotions. I knew that emotions provided good indicators of which way I should go, but they could never be the sole criterion for my decision making. This is because emotions are fickle, they can change with the moods of the given moment. I wanted whatever decision I make to withstand the test of time, regardless of the moods I might experience in the future.

Robert Spitzer, a Jesuit priest and philosopher, and president of the Spitzer Center of Ethical Leadership, explained the value of discerning the spirits and the need to follow its process in this way:

> *We make decisions every day that require good judgment and prudence, but some decisions are simply too large to be left to our judgment alone. Important life decisions – choices that set our direction in life – require spiritual discernment as well as prudence. The choice in question*

may involve a career path or a vocation; the person you marry or the role models you emulate.

The choices he listed down, and others like them, will affect our life journeys. Discernment of the spirits is essential to ensure that the decision we make is rooted in our authentic or true selves, and anchored on wisdom, good judgment, prudence, and yes, emotions too. A decision such as this will always be the right one and will stand the test of time.

One final important point before we launch into the technique of discerning the spirits. When I write about the "spirits" in this chapter, I do not mean supernatural beings, although this was part of what Ignatius contemplated within the meaning of 'spirits'. Instead I define "spirits" in the other sense that Ignatius saw them—as the inner movement in a person that drives him or her to act.

We human beings are driven by a complex set of motives in our daily choices as well as in our major decisions. What impels a boy to study to be a lawyer or a girl to want to become a scientist? Several factors contribute: their interests, desire for success, accomplishment or achievement, or to emulate a role model. Similarly, what drives a man who has chain-smoked for 10 years or a woman who is morbidly obese to become fit? Again, several factors: a need to be healthy, a desire to enjoy life with their loved ones, fear of an early death. All these factors coalesce and impel the person to act. As Joseph A. Tetlow, another Jesuit author (I will be quoting a few Jesuits in this chapter, after all, they are the experts in this process) explained, "Ignatius learned to think about those dense complexes of motives—images, ideas, attractions, and revulsions—as 'spirits'."

We can all identify spirits. There is country spirit, or patriotism, in which people feel strong love and loyalty for their

Technique Ten: Discernment of the Spirits

country. There is also fear and despair, which can grip an entire population, and exultation, which can spur an entire people to rise up. These are also what I mean when I mention "spirits" in this chapter.

Discernment through writing

Are you at a crossroads in your life? Do you face an important decision that you must make and which can impact the rest of your life and you don't know how to choose among several seemingly equally viable options? Do you feel anxious that you will choose an option that you might later regret?

Many people, who find themselves in these situations, rely only on their emotions to show them which option to take. The old cliché, 'just follow your heart' is the only decision-making tool that many people use, and the only criterion they follow is that if it feels right, then that's the way to go.

The problem with this approach is that emotions are a very unreliable basis on which to make important decisions. It is well-recognized that human beings in the throes of any strong emotions are likely to be not thinking clearly and objectively about an issue they are facing. This is why many "whirlwind romances" do not last very long. It is because couples, when they are experiencing intense feelings of love and passion toward the other person are unable to think clearly and very often make rash decisions. As these decisions are founded on very strong emotions, they tend to be easily shaken when subjected to pressurized situations.

Some people also look for signs and omens to help them make an important decision. Someone once told me that when she was deciding whether to marry a man whom she was dating, she asked for a sign from the universe in the form of a flock of birds in formation. The problem with looking for signs as basis for decision making is that if you do see the sign you've been asking for, how do you know for certain whether the universe has really given what you've asked for or you're just seeing a flock of migrating geese?

Identifying the discernment question, subjecting it to the questioning and scrutiny of reason, testing it over time, and writing about it will ensure that you make the right choice every time. Writing about the things you realize as you go through the entire discernment process is absolutely critical because it will provide you with the means to look over what has developed and changed in the course of your discernment. Your writing will provide a treasure trove of clues and indications that will reveal the correct path and show you the right decision to be made.

Key points about the discernment process

First. Trust that guidance is available to you.

Before you commence this process, it is essential to embrace the truth that the universe (or God if you believe in a divine being, or otherwise, your higher or superconscious self) wants you to achieve your good.

If you need to be guided in making a decision, then know that the Infinite Intelligence of the universe knows the right decision you must make, and the answer will be given the moment you ask for it. Knowing this, you must have faith that even if circumstances don't seem that way at the moment, everything will work out for your own good. Therefore, you should never discern about moral choices; you should never discern about something you know to be morally wrong and against your personal values and beliefs. For example, I would never recommend discernment for a person who is choosing between staying with his or her lawfully-wedded spouse and pursuing an extra-marital affair.

Technique Ten: Discernment of the Spirits

You should discern only between two or more good choices. You should seek which one is better. Discernment offers you a paradigm for making choices between several possibilities, all of which are potentially good for you.

Second. Identify the discernment question.

For instance, in my situation, I was faced with two connected discernment questions:

a. Should I leave my career as a lawyer and consider another career? and

b. Should I leave the Philippines and move to Australia?

Your discernment question might be "should I marry this person" or it could be "should I leave my job and pursue my long-dreamed of business".

Write down your discernment question when you start your Discernment of the Spirits. You should also put a date when you start, so you can refer back to it later on.

Third. Know the facts and use your reason.

Be analytical here: define the choices available to you, make a list of their pros and cons, the advantages and disadvantages, and weigh them. Write down what you realize about each available option. There are many techniques available to help you with this. When I take you through the actual technique, I will show two quick and easy tools I use myself to clarify and weigh the available options.

Fourth. Recognize your Consolations and Desolations.

Consolation is an increase in faith, hope, love and interior joy. Consolation moves us toward all these good things. It encourages us. Desolation is the opposite of consolation. One of the options we are contemplating in our decision might cause us to feel weighted down by what Ignatius described as "a darkness of the soul", a disquiet, despair and a loss of faith and love. Desolation discourages us. Pay attention to what consoles you and what makes you feel desolate and interpret them in view of your decision. Write both down. This will be explained in more detail in the actual process below.

I will explain more about Consolations and Desolations further in this chapter because of their importance; they are the foundation of the discernment of spirits.

Fifth. Test the choices either in reality or in your imagination.

Simulate in your mind what would happen if you choose one of the choices. Imagine yourself in the situation if you made each of your choices in turn. Note the feelings that rise up in each situation. Do you feel excited, passionate, joyful? Or do you feel anxious, depressed and miserable? Write down the feelings that come up as you imagine what happens after you've made each choice. Again, when I go through the actual technique with you below, I will expand on this point.

Sixth. Decide for one of the choices with time and in peace.

It's important to subject your decision through the tests of time (how did things develop in your life after you've made the decision?) and peace (did you make your decision when things were calm and peaceful in your life or when everything was chaotic?) Discernment is a process of sifting through the noise until you find what you truly long for. It is an aid to help you reach a reasoned and tested decision, as opposed to one based purely on emotion.

Technique Ten: Discernment of the Spirits

Try it yourself: Discernment of the Spirits

In Robert Frost's poem *The Road Not Taken,* the traveller was faced by two roads that diverged in the woods. Unable to see where each road led, the traveller agonized over which one to take. The traveller knew that once a choice was made, there was no turning back. The traveller eventually chose the one less travelled and trodden and it made all the difference in the traveller's life.

Discernment will help you make the choice of which road to take when you are at a crossroads in your life. Although it would be good to share your journey with someone you trust, you don't need any person to go through the discernment process with you. By chronicling and writing your experience, you can act as your own guide.

These are the seven steps of discernment:

Step 1. Identify your true desires

What do you truly desire in your life? This step involves identifying the core desires that will guide your life. Follow these guidelines to help you determine your core desire or desires:

a. Name something that you truly desire now. It can be something that you don't have yet or are already in the process of attaining.

For example, you desire to start your own business or to live and work overseas.

b. Dig deeper. Keep asking yourself "why do I want this particular desire?" And when you come up with the answer to this question, ask it again and again until you arrive at your core desire.

For example, if you desire to start your own business making a product, ask yourself why do you want this? What will it mean to you if you achieve this? The answer could be because you like being independent and you have a particular talent that you want to express.

From here, go deeper still. Ask yourself why do you want to express this particular talent? What will it mean to you if you do? When you answer this, ask the same question again. Soon, you will come to a point where you can't ask any more questions. You may realize for example, that it makes you completely happy if you create things because you are a creator.

Then you know you've arrived at a core desire. One way of knowing it's a core desire is if it will bring you good, if it will lead to your good. Do not try to explain or justify anymore why you have this core desire (this is not a psychoanalysis process). Just know that this desire is good and that you're meant to achieve it. Achieving it will lead to a fuller, happier life for you; not achieving it will result in a less fulfilling, less meaningful life for you.

Recall the times in your life when you were happiest and most at peace, when you felt consolation. What were you doing? Why did it make you happy doing what it was you were doing? This can help confirm if the core desire you identified from the above process is genuine and real.

Conversely, recall the times in your life when you felt desolation. What was happening then? What were you doing? If this is in complete contrast to the things that made you truly happy, then this can also help confirm that your core desire is genuine.

It's highly advisable that you write all your thoughts down in great detail. This step will be helpful as you now focus on the particular decision you're faced with.

Technique Ten: Discernment of the Spirits

Step 2. Use reason to weigh the options

When reason shows that one option is heavier than the other, then you should seriously consider it over the other. Use your writing to weigh and assess things. You can write down pros and cons, make listing, decision trees, tables and the like. There are two quick and easy tools I recommend. The first is a simple table:

I make Choice A		I make Choice B	
Advantages ✓	Disadvantages ✗	Advantages ✓	Disadvantages ✗

The second tool is what I call "sacred visualization", which I describe in more detail in step 3 below.

Why must we use reason, rather than feelings, to assess our options? It is because feelings, while important, are not always consistent. Brendan McManus, another Jesuit author, presents a helpful image here: that of a tidal river. Sometimes the river flows in one direction but then, with a changing of the current, it moves the opposite way. For us to successfully cross the river, we need to judge the way the current is flowing. Once we start to step into the river, we decide if we want to go with the flow of the current if it is beneficial or to resist the current if it is taking us in the wrong direction. Knowing when to resist or move with the current is the essence of wise decision-making through discernment.

To sum up, knowing our moods and inner emotional states gives us important initial information, but the second, more important, question is the direction we are moving. Be aware of your feelings and then use your head! After you reflect on the experience or decision, ask yourself:

- How do I feel about it?
- Where is this experience or decision bringing me?
- What is the likely outcome of this decision?

Knowing the answers to these questions will lead you to make a better decision.

Step 3. Consider or simulate the chosen option

Use your imagination to "virtually" experience the decision and its aftereffects. These imaginary exercises are called "contemplations" or what I call "sacred visualizations". This is no more than making use of the power of the mind to look into possibilities and how you react to them.

Bring yourself into the future after you've made your decision. What does the future look like? Are things good? How do you feel when you see this future picture – excited, encouraged and alive? Are you consoled by what you see? If the answer to all these questions is "yes", this is an indication that the choice is the right one.

You can also imagine what would happen if you do not make a particular choice. Again, jump one, three, five or ten years into the future. What does your life look like because you did not make a particular decision or you did not choose a specific path or option? Does the future look bleak? What does that image make you feel—sadness, despair, depression and discouragement? Do you feel desolation? If the answer to these questions is also yes, then it's a pretty good indication that you should have made that choice long ago.

The purpose of step 3 is to make you experience the consequences of your final decision if you actually made it and to see what your life would be like following that decision. It's like going in a flight simulator, but in your mind.

Step 4. Weigh "consolations" versus "desolations"

Step 3 will inevitably trigger feelings in you. The term "affective" refers to our feelings. Decisions can lead to affective consolations, which Ignatius described as consolations we can feel intensely or gently, or affective desolations, if we are headed the wrong way.

Your consolations or desolations are the data that you need to interpret because they are telling you about the true nature of your desire vis-à-vis the decision.

Pay attention to the consolations and understand where the desolations are coming from. Eventually, you can put aside the desolations and focus on what the consolations are saying.

It's important to point out some rules for this step:

Rule 1: be attentive to false consolations.

Follow your consolations (feelings of peace, love, joy, of being alive, excitement and passion) unless it begins to bring you long-term desolation. When that happens, stop following the seeming consolation, because it's very likely to be a false consolation. Desolation means you are moving away from your true, authentic self, the self that you were genuinely created to be. This is always a signal to re-examine any decisions or actions that might have led to the false consolations. It is usually a good idea to do this with a person or persons of wisdom, experience and maturity.

Rule 2: never make a life-changing decision in a time of desolation.

Affective desolation can impair your judgment and cause confusion and sadness. Thus, desolation will almost always lead to bad long-term life decisions. This is why Ignatius warned against making an important, potentially life-altering decision when you're experiencing desolation. He quickly added that desolation will soon give way to consolation; when this happens, you can then make better decisions. It is always worth waiting for this point.

Step 5. Subject the consolations to time and meditation

This step will require you to test the consolations by letting time pass as you meditate on them. If the consolations persist over time, then the decision has proven itself to be the right one. Take your time in this step. There is no minimum or maximum amount of time. Only you will know when you've given enough time to test your consolations.

Step 6. Make the decision

The last step is when you actually make the decision with resolve. You are also reminded to stay with the decision even if desolations come your way. The only time you should open your discernment once again is if the desolations prove to be greater than the consolations (actual ones, gained from experience) and when they persist over time. As a rule, remember Ignatius' own advice: "What you have discerned in peace, do not alter in chaos."

A story is told of an engaged woman who might have benefitted from the technique of discernment of the spirits. Her fiancé is uncomfortable talking to her about many important topics, such as beliefs, intimacy and money. She too is keeping certain things about herself secret from him. There is a sense of uneasiness, disquiet and, often, agitation in their relationship. She can see many warning signs, but chooses to ignore them. Despite all these red flags, she believes marrying him is the right thing to do because "something still feels right" about it.

The problem is that the wedding date has been set. Contracts have been signed, venues booked and money paid. Marriage is not going to suddenly and miraculously cause them to start opening up to each other or uncover what they're hiding from one another. This woman could really benefit from someone, like a spiritual director, going through the discernment of the spirts with her and pointing out the warning signs that she chooses not to see. This process will make her see how her feelings are leading her astray and pulling her away from her true self. Had she subjected her decision and "tested the spirits" she would have clearly seen that going ahead with the marriage will lead to long-term desolation instead of consolation.

Signs and landmarks

For about six months, I went through the exact same steps I described above. All throughout, my constant companion was my thick, leather bound journal and my pen. I wrote down everything that I went through, all my thoughts, feelings, realizations ("eureka" moments), as well as questions and answers.

I thought that the discernment process would only help me make the right decision, but it did more than that. It allowed me to discover who I really was, what motivated and moved me to think and act the way I did, and taught me more about myself than any counsellor or psychologist ever could. The product of that process was the firm decision to leave my life, my family, friends, job and career in the Philippines, and start a new life in Australia. It is a decision that through the years has proven to be correct in every respect.

When you have a sincere desire to find an answer to your question and commit yourself to this process, you will have an unshakable sense that you are being guided by an external power, and it is guiding you both from within and without. You will also know that you are moving along the right direction because you will reach certain signs or landmarks. Earlier, I wrote about how signs are an unreliable basis for decision making. This has been true in my experience and in others' experiences too. Something that I was so sure was a sign that I should head in a particular direction or do a certain action turned out to be completely wrong. Taken by themselves, signs are unreliable; but when they appear in the course of your discernment journey, they can provide you rich clues that you are on the right path. You must chronicle what happens to and around you when you see these signs or reach these landmarks. They will form part of your "blueprint", which you can refer back to later on should you be faced with another important decision that needs to be made.

One of the signs and landmarks you might experience is an increase in self-knowledge, consolations and peace. The process of discernment will allow you to look and enquire within as you determine what is important to you. As you continue to dig deep at your motivations, you will discover many things about yourself that you never knew before. As you continuously weigh one option against another, you might find that one option consoles you more, and you sense an increasing feeling of peace that this option is the right one to choose. You must remember to write about this because your writing will serve as an anchor later on when the inevitable storms of conflict and challenge come. Your writing will serve as a powerful reminder that you have repeatedly tested your decision and you know it's the right one, and no matter what temporary turbulence arises as a result, you will abide by what you have decided.

Technique Ten: Discernment of the Spirits

Typically accompanying this increasing sense of peace is a quiet or sublime indifference to the ultimate outcome of your decision. Remember that you embarked on your entire discernment process believing that you are guided by God (in whatever way, shape or form you believe God to be), who cares for you in a deeply intimate and personal way. As your discernment is set on this strong foundation, you develop the conviction that no matter what happens to you and your life as a result of your decision, everything will work out in the end for your good. You start to possess an unshakable belief that ultimately, you will be all right, and all will be well.

You may also start seeing a convergence of circumstances confirming to you that a particular option you are considering is the right one. This could come in the form of serendipitous events and circumstances that favor you and your plans. You may start experiencing what analytical psychologist Carl Jung described as 'synchronicity' and start seeing coincidences taking place in your life that are seemingly unconnected to one another, but are meaningful when considered in light of the important decision you are discerning.

The final and perhaps the strangest and most wonderful landmark in your discernment is what is called 'the mystical moment'. On writing this, I debated whether I should use an alternate, more secular, less spiritual term, but I think it will lessen how truly miraculous this landmark really is. It is the moment when you know, absolutely and indubitably, with all the certainty in the universe, that the decision you have made is the true and correct one.

The mystical moment can happen any time, usually when you least expect it, and can come in the form you least expect. I described one of the most powerful mystical moments I've ever experienced in my life in Chapter 8. This happened when I gazed upon the sun setting over the Yarra River in Melbourne, which happened to be the exact same scene shown on the photo I had cut out and pasted on my computer monitor when I first set the intention of living in Australia.

As of the time of writing, that was 14 years ago. Since I discerned the spirits and made that original decision that took me to Australia, I have never had any reason to look back. In that time, I've experienced some of the highest highs and the lowest lows of my life. But not once did I think that I had made the wrong decision.

The decision that I had made after I had gone through discernment has withstood the tests of time and everything else that the world could throw at it. It has never been shaken. I've experienced many consolations and desolations since making that original decision. But the consolations far outweigh the desolations; and what's more, the desolations all passed, as they always do, while the consolations have lasted. All told, this is how I know that the decision I had made all those years ago was the right one.

Technique Eleven: Love letters to and from a future beloved

Call out to your perfect mate using pen and paper

While I've used all the techniques that I teach in this book to achieve the higher good in different aspects of my life, it's the next technique that I'm going to teach that has turned my world upside down. It has created for me the most joy and contentment because it brought me something that, at one point, was my heart's deepest desire. The technique I'll show in this chapter is what I used to attract the perfect mate. Applying this technique allowed me to manifest the relationship of my dreams. It is also what has allowed me to be in a wonderful relationship with my beautiful partner Antonella for more than six years now.

So, brace yourselves because this is the chapter where things will get slightly melodramatic; a lump will form in my throat and I'll get a bit teary-eyed as I tell the following story.

Wishing versus Receiving

"There is a difference between wishing for a thing and being ready to receive it," Napoleon Hill, author of *Think and Grow Rich*, wrote.

This struck me. At first, reading what he wrote made no sense to me. What's the difference between wishing or desiring something and being ready to receive it? When we want something, aren't we also ready to get it? To receive it? Aren't these two ideas the same?

I didn't know then, but I do now, that many wishes and desires go unfulfilled because the person wishing or desiring has not placed him or herself in a position to receive the thing asked for. I learned this most valuable lesson after I met Antonella in August 2014.

I arrived at the Sydney Aquarium café a half hour early for my date. I was meeting Antonella for the first time in person. We had agreed to meet at 10 a.m. but I was so nervous that that decided to come early just so I could calm down if needed.

I knew it was her the moment I saw her walking outside toward the café. If I was being honest with myself, her photos didn't do her justice. She looked even more radiant and beautiful than her photos.

"Hello, Jonathan?" she asked with a warm smile. Her Italian accent back then was still as thick as béchamel.

"Yes, Antonella? I replied.

"Yes," she replied, accepting my all too enthusiastically-offered handshake.

"It's lovely to meet you," I said, noting that she was still smiling. *Hey maybe I won't mess this up this time,* I thought to myself.

That was how we met. The circumstances of our meeting were typical of how many other couples meet—a first date, over coffee, on a lazy Saturday morning. But the means that allowed us to meet were atypical. I am convinced that she entered my world because I was finally ready for the kind of love and commitment that I had desired for so long, but which I was not, up to that point, truly ready to receive.

Technique Eleven: Love letters to and from a future beloved

We talked as we strolled around Darling Harbour on that perfect winter morning. I noted the fact that I immediately felt at ease with her. Even though her first language was Italian, I also noted, with pleasant surprise, that I didn't have to exert any effort in our conversation. I saw these as very good signs. I was also immediately attracted to her Mediterranean beauty.

As far as I could tell, she seemed genuinely interested to learn about me; and it didn't seem that she was appalled by my physical appearance. She was talking about her life so far in Australia, where she was from in Italy, her family – all the usual safe, but important topics, on a first date.

We had breakfast at a restaurant overlooking a picturesque section of Darling Harbour. Before I knew it, it was almost one o'clock p.m. and she had to go. I had known within two minutes of meeting her that I wanted to see her again. I asked to see her again as we parted ways at the end of our date. And to my delight, she agreed to meet me the very next weekend.

As I write these words, it has been six years since our first date. But my memory of that morning, and how we got together, remains crisp in my mind, as if it happened last week. I recall that long before that first meeting, I had written a letter addressed to God asking Him to give me the gift of "big love". I got what I asked for, but it took a while. It took years in fact. More than anything else, this experience demonstrated to me the importance of preparation and patience while waiting for a prayer to be answered.

Writing the first letters

The idea of writing down what I want as an indispensable step to getting it was not new to me. But I had never used it before to bring in people to my experience. As in other times, it took a gentle nudge from an external source to remind me that writing can certainly be used to reshape reality and draw in the people, circumstances, and things that delight us. Again, it was Henriette Klauser's *Write It Down, Make It Happen* book that spurred me to write letters to an imaginary, soon-to-be-met, partner. I took cues from her case study on Gloria and used her story as a guide to the process of writing to attract a mate.

In Part One where I told my story of writing, I described how I created a "Think and Decree" notebook in mid-2006 with the intention of writing in there all the things and experiences I wanted to create in my world. The first entry I wrote was that I wanted to work, live and establish ties in Australia. And when I finally arrived five months after writing this intention, I wrote my second entry that I wanted to share all the wonderful experiences I knew was going to have in my new home country with someone in a loving, committed long-term relationship.

Desiring to meet a particular person to be in a long-term relationship with (and this is not just limited to romantic personal relationships, but also includes other social, professional and business relationships) falls under what I call "experiencing" goals (the other types of goals being "having" and "being" goals). I have always found these goals the most difficult to aim for and achieve because it's not something you can control or orchestrate. You can order and buy a car or a house or a vacation; but you can't really order or buy a relationship, at least not a genuine one.

I read a story once of how a woman who desired to have children wrote letters to their souls, long before they were born, to draw them to her. This was a strange, unheard of idea for me; it delved into spiritual realms that I did not understand or dare enter.

Still, this technique of drawing in a person to our experience deeply resonated with me. It made sense in a way I couldn't explain. I thought there was nothing to lose by writing letters to my future partner. I adapted this technique to my own circumstances and

Technique Eleven: Love letters to and from a future beloved

began writing my own "soulmate" letters. This was the first step that would later lead me to a tipping point.

What this exercise did for me was to get me to feel how real it would be to have this person in my life. As I began writing the letters, the feeling of being in a committed, loving, long-term relationship started becoming more and more natural to me. In time, the feelings took on a sense of realism. Although there was no evidence that she was anywhere on the horizon, I knew it was only a matter of time before she came. I just needed to be patient.

My first letter started awkwardly, but sincerely, with hopeful expectation:

> *My dear Soulmate,*
>
> *It's 6 o'clock in the morning here. What time is it where you are? I don't know how I know this, but I feel that you are here now in this country too. You are near me, looking at the same sky and sunrise as I am. It's beautiful here isn't it? I think it's only appropriate that I meet the love of my life in the home I've chosen for the other half of my life. Do you know that I feel that God is guiding my paths and decisions here largely with you in mind? Yes, my love, He's already factored you into the equation of my life. God is good because He's involved even (or should I say, especially) in my love life. And He should be involved. You, after all, are the greatest blessing He has given me. If he was involved in the lesser details of my life, all the more that He'll be involved in getting us together. In the current equation of my life, you are the factor that will bring me the greatest joy and happiness.*

I acknowledged that I had closed one chapter of my life by leaving home and choosing to relocate to another country. If I was to usher in new significant relationships, I knew that I needed to release old ones that no longer served me. I needed to create space for what was to come:

> *I feel that I'm now reaching the point where I've finally closed the door to my past. I know my heart is now open to for you to enter. You are the good that will fill the void in my life, the void that I've created.*

As I finished writing this letter, I settled into a feeling of calm, certain knowing that what I was writing was somehow finding its way to the intended receiver:

> *I look at the sky slowly and gently brighten with the rising of the sun. It makes me happy to know that you are looking at the same sky as I am.*

Whatever the reason or the season

I don't blame you if you find it difficult to grasp the concept that simply writing letters to imaginary persons, without doing anything else, would draw them in to your world. To be fair, although I wrote letters mostly, there were other things that I wrote too (see below in Helpful steps). I also did actions when I was inspired to do so like going out and meeting people in a spirit of genuine curiosity and light-heartedness.

Mostly, however, I wrote letters. I wrote for a whole lot of reasons. I wrote letters to crystallize my wishes, to tell the person upstairs, the Big Cahuna, what I wanted in a woman and in a relationship. Not for one moment did I believe that God was like a waiter in a restaurant waiting passively for me to peruse the menu and make my order. Instead, I specified what I wanted because

Technique Eleven: Love letters to and from a future beloved

I believed whatever I wanted was within the capacity of Infinite Power to deliver to me. I was participating in the creative laboratory that was my own life.

In some letters, I even tried seeing and feeling from the side of the beloved:

> *My dear Soulmate,*
>
> *Do you feel me coming closer and closer to you? I feel it, and I'm certain that you do too. You were born and raised in Australia or you could have been born here, raised abroad and returned home. Why do I know this? I don't know exactly. I guess it's only fitting that the love of my life will come from the country that I've decided to embrace as my home for the remainder of my life.*
>
> *We will be united soon. Feel me coming into your life very soon and thank the Lord, as I always do, for bringing us together.*

When things were looking stormy and gloomy in terms of my prospects of ever meeting this person, I wrote letters to her, and other times to God or the Universe or Infinite Intelligence (see *Chapter Seven Calling S.O.S. to the Universe*) asking them what was taking so damned long:

> *Oh my love where are you? What's taking you so long to come to me? It was so very hard to lift my pen and write to you, because I wasn't sure if you'd hear me. But what else can I do but pour out my longing for you in this journal. I refuse to give in to despair and hopelessness concerning your arrival. I want to hang on with faith, believing you'll really come. This is all I can do now.*

Looking back at these early letters, it is clear that my impatience was being magnified by the inactivity in all other areas of my life in Australia back then. I was alone and isolated in a new country and I projected my loneliness and my desperation on to my letters:

> *I've been feeling especially lonely these past few days. I've been longing for you. If I could only put all this loneliness and longing in a bottle and cast it out to sea. Then I'd be rid of it. But I can't do that and so I struggle with this loneliness.*
>
> *Please come to me. Don't make me wait too long for you. I feel like crying now. Honestly I do. Because I have no one to share my life with here. I have no one to share my small victories with, no one to laugh and walk with, no one to sing and dream with. I want to share all these things with you.*
>
> *God, please hear the cry of my heart and send me my soulmate. I have faith that I'm ready to receive her now. Really I am. Please let this be the time when she'll finally come and enter my life.*

I truly had no concept then that saying I was ready to receive someone was different from being ready to receive someone. There was a gulf between them. I could not possibly be in a position to receive this person as long as I was feeling empty inside. There was also a difference between creating a void in your life so that the universe could fill it with something good, and feeling empty, exhausted, and spent within.

> *My heart is a little tired of being disappointed and of waiting. I've never had a relationship go the distance.*

How I envy people who say they've been with their partners for 4 years, 6 years…forever. Why can't I have that? My heart is tired, it's true. I've tried looking, but I've been frustrated and disappointed time and again. I can't assert my own will in this matter.

Writing through to resolution

I kept writing. The empty piece of white paper became my port, my safe harbor. Within its confines, I could control what happened and be secure. I had no control over the weather outside, but on that piece of paper, I could make the sun shine all day if I wanted to. It became a place where I could leave my doubts, anxieties and fears.

I realized early on that the key was to write these letters to my beloved the way I'd actually be writing them if she were actually already around. I knew that if anything great happened in my day or if I scored any minor or major victories, the first thing I'd do if I had a partner was tell her about it. So, I wrote these letters too, thinking that she would read them somehow:

> *My dearest wife,*
>
> *In you, God has given me the greatest prosperity blessing. You are my faith made concrete, my vision finally made real.*
>
> *Oh we'll have such amazing times together. We'll do a lot of travelling throughout our lives together. By the time we're both old and grey, we'll be singing the Beatles' song I really love: "You and I have memories, longer than the road that stretches out ahead."*
>
> *Come to me now my love. I'm waiting eagerly for your coming.*

Helpful steps

Writing these letters allowed me to feel that being with a partner was something real. Frequently, as I wrote these letters, I felt hope welling within me that this simple act of writing a letter was somehow causing effects which, though invisible to me, were very real.

Apart from writing these letters, I wrote other things though to help clarify exactly what I wanted and keep my level of expectation up, and as an antidote to impatience and doubt.

I made a short and simple list of qualities I wanted my partner to have. This helped me clarify my intentions more effectively and I believe more powerfully than a long-drawn out description ever could.

In all, there were 25 items in my list of qualities I wanted in an ideal partner. I was very specific when it came to the inner qualities and characteristics I wanted my woman to have (for example, must be kind and gentle, wise, God-fearing). I was also specific with the feelings I wanted her to make me feel (for example, someone who makes me feel good about myself and the world, who keeps me positive). But I wasn't caught up at all on other specifics like physical appearance (apart from a general requirement that she look after her health and well-being), what she did for a living, ethnicity, religion, etc. I let God sort out these other details.

Henriette Klauser explained that when we don't list down the things we want, we remain vague and general. We stay safe. When we are generalized and safe, nothing can happen and nothing changes. With this in mind, I also listed down some of the things that I needed in order to be happy in a relationship with my future partner. I wasn't picky here at all, simply listing 10 things: for example, in my relationship—

Technique Eleven: Love letters to and from a future beloved

- "I need to feel valued and respected";
- "I need to feel inspired by my partner to become a better person";
- "I need to know that she is inspired by me to become a better person herself"; and
- "I need to feel wanted by her and passionately desired by her".

After writing this list, I granted myself each item on my list by writing it as an affirmation. So, each of the examples above became affirmations as follows:

- I value and respect myself;
- I inspire myself constantly to become a better person;
- I possess the gift of inspiring my woman to be a better person; and
- I am wanted and passionately desired by my woman.

I learned this last listing technique from a book titled *Calling in 'the One': 7 Weeks to Attract the Love of Your Life* by Katherine Woodward Thomas. Although I was unsure about this book at first when I read the title, I am a big follower of other teachers who teach the power of writing as a tool to transform ourselves, our lives and worlds. I'm always on the lookout for other teachers' books and programs and keen to "test drive" their methods to see if they work. I consider Katherine's book, and the teachings and lessons contained in it, to be the final thing that tipped the scales in my favor in my relationship search. Her book is the real deal.

Following some of my own techniques (see *Chapter 2 Writing to the 100th Power* and *Chapter 5 Gratitude listing*), I rewrote these lists regularly and gave thanks in writing that I had already received what I wanted. When I grew impatient or doubtful that things were changing, I wrote my lists to refocus my energy (see *Chapter 1 Mind Your Energy*) and remind me that what I had asked for was on its way—that she was on her way. I looked at my lists regularly whenever I found myself losing heart. I willed myself to remember that my lists described what was waiting for me. My writing gave me something concrete to see and believe in.

Make believe words

In July, my beloved wrote to me. I put on paper all that I longed to hear her say to me.

> *My darling Jonathan,*
>
> *Since God caused our two separate paths to cross, I have never ceased thanking Him for answering my prayer and bringing you into my life. For truly, that is what you are—no more and no less than heaven's answer to my heart's deepest prayer and my soul's deepest longing.*
>
> *You are a gift to me, living proof that there is love that awaits those who wait in faith for it.*
>
> *I love all of you. I love you for your strength and passion. I love you for your faith and patience. I love you for your courage. I love your ability to embrace me constantly with such boundless love I've never known before. I love your creativity and your thoughtfulness. I love your wit, your charm and sense of humor. I love your positivity and optimism in life; and need I say, I love your sexiness and handsome good looks.*

Technique Eleven: Love letters to and from a future beloved

I love the way you make me feel as a woman. With you, I feel beautiful, desired, loved, ravished, adored. I love the way you make me feel as a lover—wanted, lusted after, consumed. I love the way you make me feel as a wife—respected, honored, cherished. I love the way you make me feel as the mother of our children—treasured, secured, protected. I love the way you make me feel as a partner and friend—thoughtfully considered, sought after, needed.

One of my favorite lines from the Bible says that "a good wife is a gift from heaven; her value is far beyond pearls." You've told me many times how I am a gift from heaven, and how you value me second only to our God. But the converse of this passage from scripture is likewise true: "a good husband is a gift from the Lord; his value is far more than his weight in gold."

You are my greatest treasure, Jonathan Olavides Temporal. I invite you to walk through life with me, to love with me, to laugh and play with me, to nurture me. It brings me much happiness to think that I am your woman—fully, completely and totally yours.

My soul rejoices without tiring when I see us loving and sharing life, raising our children, building our family, going on holidays together, celebrating birthdays, anniversaries and countless other joyous occasions together, and above all, growing old together.

I love and cherish you my dear husband. With you, my heart has finally found its forever hiding place. Yours always

With love,

Your beloved

More than any other letter, it was this one that did it for me: it made me truly feel that she was not just on the way, but she had already arrived and I would soon prove this as indisputable fact. Unlike my earlier letters, I wrote this letter from a place of peace, joy and contentment.

In the early months of our relationship, Antonella had occasion to tell me, more than once, that "I was a gift to her'". I was not surprised to hear her say the actual words that I had written in my imaginary letter. When I read it, it felt so real to the point that when she eventually said these words to me, I was convinced that she had already said them before through her letter.

The most important step: Letting go

When we desire something deeply and have done everything we can to get it, and still end up empty-handed, then it's time to release what we desire. In doing so, we must trust that the Universe has already acted on our desire and already brought it to us. Ten months before Antonella entered my life, I wrote this letter to God.

> *I now realize that it is this very desire, this longing that is keeping my soulmate from finally manifesting. It is this need for a partner that is keeping me from becoming free.*
>
> *I now ask for your spirit to help me completely and totally surrender my desire and need to have and find a partner. I lovingly put to rest this desire in your hands and entrust it to your care. Purify my heart, release it from all attachments — mental, emotional, spiritual — to women, especially the love, affection and companionship of a woman.*

Technique Eleven: Love letters to and from a future beloved

> *Finally, I ask you to give me true inner peace, happiness and contentment. Let me be truly and deeply happy in my own skin, in my own life. Allow me to focus my attention and devote all my energies to achieving my dreams. As I do this, fill my heart with love and wash me with your peace. The peace that goes beyond all human understanding.*
>
> *I feel your peace now, even as I write these words. And so it is.*

A few months after I wrote the above letter, I was on vacation. I was relaxing in my apartment alone. I was doing boring, mundane housework and was perfectly happy and content doing it. I had just taken my clothes from the washing machine and was hanging them out to dry on the balcony. A cool wind was blowing through the trees just beyond my balcony. I stopped for a moment, enjoying the stillness around me. I felt at peace.

And then, just then, I sensed something stir inside me. The sensation was so subtle, like a whisper, yet so clear.

You will meet your soulmate soon. She is coming.

I sensed it and felt it. I didn't get all excited or anything when I had this sensation. I just stayed relaxed and at peace. I smiled and silently thanked God for whispering this beautiful message into my spirit. Although I released it at that moment, the promise stayed with me throughout the whole weekend and for a long time after that.

Three months after this episode on the balcony, and almost at the same time as I started writing with deliberate intention, Antonella entered my world. We met for the first time in person a few weeks after. When I was truly ready and in a place where I could receive this kind of relationship and be in a position to give the kind of commitment it needed, things happened almost instantaneously and effortlessly on my part. But every day that I am with her reminds me that to get to this place of readiness meant literally years of waiting and preparing on my part.

As of this writing, I am living what I have asked for, for almost six years now. Our life together has been blissful, interrupted only occasionally by the challenges that most adult relationships go through, and frequently punctuated by moments of indescribable delight and humble thanksgiving.

Someone once told me that when something you've been waiting for so long finally arrives, it will be worth every moment you waited; experiencing its presence in your life will wipe away the memory of the many years of waiting. I thought this a bit too cliché. I swore that when my day finally came, when I told my family and friends about my new relationship, and they ask me how I got to be so lucky, I wouldn't do anything as uncouth as answering in clichés. But there is a reason why things become clichéd, and that's because they are true.

When it finally happened for me, when big love finally came, all I could do was spout out a few familiar clichés—"it was worth the wait", "all good things come to those who wait" and "lucky in life, lucky in love" being on top of my list. I look forward to reciting many more of these clichés as I continue to live my life with my beloved.

What's particularly awe-inspiring and humbling for me was realizing that what happened after I wrote those letters was no accident and that, somehow, I had a direct hand in creating all of it. There is no way I can explain in any logical, rational or scientific sense how or why many of the things I had asked for came to me. For instance, in one letter, of my future partner, I had written:

Technique Eleven: Love letters to and from a future beloved

> *You could have been born here, raised abroad and returned home.*

This was an uncannily accurate description of Antonella's life. She was born in Wollongong, Australia, moved with her family back to Italy when she was just six years old, and she came back to Australia a few months before we met. And then again, in another letter, this time with me writing from my imaginary partner's point of view and pretending that she was the one writing these words to me, I wrote:

> *You are a gift to me, living proof that there is love that awaits those who wait in faith for it.*

After Antonella and I started dating, imagine my surprise when she wrote me a card in which she described me as "the gift" that her nonna (grandmother) promised her would one day come. There are many other examples of things about my future partner that I had written and had asked for that were in fact later granted in the person of Antonella. Like I wrote all those years ago, I cannot explain how this happened. And I'm fine with that. I don't feel the need to explain it. That takes all the fun out of it. I'd rather happily swim in the mystery of this inexplicable and indecipherable process of co-creation without ever understanding the how's and the why's of it all.

Try the technique yourself: writing letters to and from a future beloved

Writing a detailed description of your desire sends a clear message to yourself that it's possible and you are ready to receive it. Writing allows you to name it, claim it, believe it and finally receive it. So be specific when you describe your desire. The more specific your description, the readier you are to receive. Write a description in loving detail, of what your goal would be like and what your everyday life will be like once this goal is yours.

If your goal is to find a loving partner and be in a committed, long-term relationship, write letters to her or him. Write these letters as a way of helping you feel how real it could be for you.

If things are taking too long and you are feeling doubtful, impatient, even desperate, ask, through your writing, what lessons you need to learn from this experience of waiting? What do you need to do to perfect yourself during this period of necessary waiting? Realize that the vision you have been given of a life of loving togetherness with someone will come in its appointed time and will not be late. Just sit tight and record your musings.

Then, when you least expect it, the beloved you've waited for will come.

Technique Twelve: Creating solid self-confidence

Recall past victories and acknowledge present wins to create rock hard self-belief

Recall what was taught way back in Chapter 1 that minding your mental energy and focusing it only on the outcomes you want, is key to achieving big goals, solving vexing problems, and shaping your life. In other words, thought control is critical to achieve success in your plans.

It is impossible to control the thousands of thoughts running freely in our minds every minute throughout the day. That's why we have to use deliberate and intentional techniques to rein our thoughts in as much as possible. Writing is one of the best and most potent ways to do this.

Much has also been written about the important link between thoughts and feelings. We've all had days when we're feeling we're on top of the world. And we've all had days too when we're feeling so bad, all we want to do is crawl under a rock and hide out there for a while. If we want to move forward, it is critically important that we pump ourselves up and feel we can achieve big things. And nothing can pump us better than by remembering the many times in the past when we won. Nothing will galvanize thoughts and feelings and direct them toward positive directions more than reminding ourselves that we are already winners.

Affirm and build on past successes

The end of 2015 to the first quarter of 2016 was a period of great triumph, shattering disappointment and progressive personal transition for me. In a 7-month span, I became a lawyer in Australia, graduated with a Master of Business degree from one of Australia's leading business schools (a huge goal I had set for myself three years prior), got my first job as a lawyer in a Sydney law firm, was fired (or more accurately, got myself fired) from that firm within five months and took on a $40,000 debt. What a year!

In that brief list, I count three victories and two defeats (well maybe one, depending on how you look at borrowing $40,000 just before losing your job). Even though the victories outnumbered the defeats, it was the defeats that stayed in my mind for many days and nights. I had never been fired from a job in my life; all the previous law firms and employers I had as a lawyer were all sad and sorry to see me leave them at one point and did their best to get me to stay. To be fired by an employer in my field where I had prided myself as being excellent in was a mortifying slap in the face. Never mind that I would have left that firm sooner rather than later, but for them to tell me that I wasn't good enough for them was a humiliating blow.

The thing with defeats is that they tend to stick more in our memories rather than victories. What we once considered amazing victories and breakthrough successes in time tend to be trivialized. But defeats and losses often don't become minimized in our minds. Instead, we play and replay the defeats in our minds and think, "well maybe if I had done this or that, the outcome would have been different and I would have won". Have you ever wished that you had a time machine to take you back to the moment just before

Technique Twelve: Creating solid self-confidence

you suffered a crushing defeat so that you could undo your actions and bring about a victorious result? I know I have done this many times.

After spending the next several days walking around in a daze and sitting in bed at night wondering how on earth I was going to get another job in a hyper competitive job market and pay off a new $40,000 personal loan, I decided enough was enough. I followed my gut instinct to leap out of my comfort zone and do actions out of courage and not fear. One of the things I did was sign up for Jack Canfield's Success Coaching Program. The program cost USD$5,000. I debated in my mind countless times whether I could afford to join this program and pay an amount that, when converted to Australian dollars, was about 17% of my personal loan, and whether I should instead be saving this money for the lean months that I was sure would follow for me and my beautiful partner. At that time, she also didn't have a full-time job.

Joining Jack Canfield's coaching program was one of the best decisions I could have ever made at that point in my life. It encouraged me to ignore the seeming reality of my present circumstances and dream bigger. It forced me to turn away from my pressing worries and look forward to turning my situation around.

One of the things I learned from the coaching program was how important it was to recall all my successes, both recent victories and lifetime achievements. I learned how vital it was to write and list down my victories and keep a record of my successes during the day in a daily victory log. The practice alone of writing down my successes stopped me from losing hope.

I divided my life into three equal periods and listed down the three major victories I achieved in each of those periods. To complete this process, I had to sift through all the times in my life when I was successful at something or achieved a successful outcome. As I started writing down my nine major victories, I quickly realized that I had more successes than I had failures. I believe it will be the same for you and many others. But like me, I suspect that you will at first focus on your failures more than your successes. Why does the human brain do this?

I see this as an evolutionary survival trait. Negative experiences always cause some degree of pain to us, be it physical, emotional, psychological or a combination of all of these. Negative experiences are unpleasant. So, it's natural for our brains to want to avoid something unpleasant, something that is painful. Our brains tend to remember negative experiences because if we forget them easily, we may endanger our survival by not seeing the danger signs. Being sensitive to negative cues warns us to be alert and prepared.

Failure often brings a slew of strong negative emotions, which are impressed upon the brain. The brain remembers how bad we felt when we suffered from a relationship breakdown, lost a job, experienced bereavement, or got made redundant. And yet the brain doesn't tend to create the same level of intense positive emotions around our successes. The result is that when we experience a setback, our confidence, self-esteem and self-trust take a hit. Many of us may even get stuck in the rut of perfectionism—the feeling that even if we've already achieved success in something, it's still not good enough; our performance has to be faultless and our results flawless for us to be content.

Being stuck in the trap of perfectionism hinders us from savoring the journey toward achieving our goals. This stops us from simply enjoying life. As we remember how this experience or that experience was less than perfect and rehash the bad feelings when we got less than successful results, it dampens our enthusiasm and makes us shy away from giving things another try and taking risks that are essential to achieve big goals.

Technique Twelve: Creating solid self-confidence

When you begin to recall past successes and acknowledge to yourself that you achieved the best performance or result, and how far you've come in regard to a current goal, your confidence, belief and trust in yourself and your abilities grow.

It takes some effort at first to recall past victories; once you start doing it, however, it comes naturally and easily, and you feel splendid as you immerse yourself in the feelings of success, jubilation and pride that you felt when you were actually celebrating a past victory. With the self-confidence and self-trust that comes from knowing that you faced tough situations in the past and emerged victorious, you become more courageous at going after big goals. In time, you become successful again. Your successes will stack up, and you'll build unstoppable momentum as you hurtle toward new and even bigger goals.

Daily wins

When Facebook Chief Operating Officer Sheryl Sandberg lost her husband Dave Goldberg suddenly and unexpectedly in 2015, she lost hope that she and her children would ever again be happy and that they would every feel pure joy again. But it wasn't just hope that she lost. "When Dave died, my confidence crumbled overnight," she wrote.

In a dark period, she called her friend, psychologist Adam Grant, because she believed her grief would never end and she needed help. Grant helped Sandberg see that grief runs its course and that life does and will get better. Grant showed her that it's by having faith that things will one day look up, that things won't always be bad and that life will get better, and taking daily steps carrying this conviction that people build resilience. He also taught her the concrete steps that everyone can take to recover and rebound from loss.

Together, they wrote *Option B*, a book that recounts Sandberg's personal insights and combines them with Grant's revealing research on people finding strength in the midst of adversity. They also recounted their insights in a short LinkedIn course titled *Build Resilience in the Face of Adversity*.

I was immediately drawn to the message of *Option B*. Losing a loved one such as a spouse, parent or child is perhaps the deepest, most significant and painful loss humans will encounter in life. In a very real sense, it is the worst defeat that we can ever experience. When my father died suddenly when I was 21 years old, I was numb for months after. Like Sandberg, I was convinced that neither I nor my family would ever feel whole again. And yet my and my family's hearts healed in time and one day, unexpectedly, we found that we could again feel joy.

I immediately saw the power in the techniques that Grant and Sandberg taught in *Option B*, because they helped people recover and rebound from the worst of human experiences. And if techniques like these helped people overcome this deep level of defeat, then surely, they would help in getting over lesser defeats.

One of the techniques that Grant taught Sandberg to overcome adversity, restore self-confidence and build resilience was journaling. She wrote in *Option B* that there is research suggesting that journaling can be really helpful in restoring self-confidence in the midst of bereavement. From my own experience, this is one hundred per cent true.

Grant told her to write down every night before she went to bed the three things she did well that day. Even though at first, she felt she had nothing to put on the list, she started doing it anyway. During the first few nights, she wrote down things she did well during the day, like making tea or going through a meeting without crying or at least without crying a lot. To some people, these might

Technique Twelve: Creating solid self-confidence

be trivial, insignificant acts. But for her, given what she was going through, these acts represented small wins.

After some time doing this exercise, something in Sandberg clicked. "When I went to bed writing three things I did well, what I realized is that even before Dave had died, I went to bed every night worrying about what I did wrong," she recounted. "Now I've told lots of people to do this, and lots of my friends have written down three things they do well, and it is transformative. I don't think I realized how much time I spent beating myself up for things that went wrong rather than focusing on the things that went well."

In the next few months, Sandberg unexpectedly experienced brief moments of joy. She recounted a time when she very briefly felt joy. She was dancing with a girl friend at a bar mitzvah four months after her husband died. "And for like a minute it was just amazing, and then I literally burst into tears on the dance floor. At first, I didn't know what was wrong," she recounted.

She then realized that she had felt joy for one minute and was quickly overcome by guilt. "I immediately felt so guilty that I felt any happiness, any joy, that I just crumbled."

At this point, Grant helped Sandberg take back joy. He gave her another suggestion: write down three moments of joy every night. Sandberg explained: "Every night before I go to bed, I write down three moments of joy. And they can be really small. But what happens is that because I'm noticing those three moments of joy, it makes the whole day more joyful. And I think anyone who's gone through trauma, knowing that it is okay to find joy is so important."

Without expecting it, she had tapped into the subtle, wonderful power of writing to change our inner states. The simple act of writing down before going to bed the three things she did well caused her to focus on small wins, and this ultimately helped restore her self-confidence and build her resilience in the face of adversity. And listing down three moments of joy every night helped her reclaim the joy that she believed she had forever lost after her husband died.

Turbo charging your success list

As you might probably have realized by now, I like writing lists. Sometimes, I like writing long lists. When the need calls for it, I don't leave anything in my mind and instead leave everything out on paper.

The technique I learned from Jack Canfield of writing down my nine major life successes certainly worked. At a low point in my life, I needed to be reminded that I wasn't a loser but a winner. And I needed to remind myself constantly of this fact.

When life throws you a curve ball and you need a gentle reminder that you are still successful despite a setback, then it's ok to list down your nine major life successes. But in my case, in the autumn of 2016, I needed more than a gentle, subtle reminder that I had been successful in the past and that this was just a temporary setback.

No, I needed a jolt, a bucketful of water poured over my head. I needed to be reminded in a massive way that no matter how low I fell, and no matter what other people thought of me or what they did to me, that I was a winner and that I had won so many times in my life. I needed it rubbed in my face that I was a conqueror and that I had stepped up and conquered so many seemingly unconquerable challenges in my life. I needed to massage my ego that I was a victor, that even though I had lost before, I always managed to find a way to emerge victorious.

So, I took the nine major successes technique and I supercharged it. I endeavored to list down the 101 successes in my life. As I wrote down each of the 101 greatest successes in my life,

Technique Twelve: Creating solid self-confidence

I reminded myself that I am already a greatly successful person and that I am succeeding in life.

Writing the first 10 or 15 successes was easy; I bet most of us can count this many number of wins by the time we were 20 years old. But after listing down my 25th or 30th victory, I found it wasn't as easy to list down my other successes – and I still had 70 to go!

It was at this point when I realized something. To be considered a "success" in my life, worthy of being added to my 101 list, it didn't always have to be a massive victory, it didn't need to be an amazing, spectacular achievement. Yes, I listed down those types of successes too. Certainly, it's nice to remind ourselves that we've had massive wins in the past. But I also realized that it's also ok to list things that demonstrate that we're moving closer to a goal.

Earl Nightingale, in his audio recording *The Strangest Secret*, defined success as "the progressive realization of a worthy ideal". He said that to the extent that a person was moving closer to a worthy ideal he or she set for himself or herself, to the extent that a person is getting closer to achieving a worthwhile goal, then that person is successful.

I've had many worthwhile goals in my life. And I've achieved many of them. Following Earl Nightingale's definition, every time I did a significant act or achieved a result that brought me closer to a goal, then I was already successful. That act or outcome then went on my list. From that point onwards, coming up with success number 31 to 101 was easier.

Success for each person is relative to your age, experience, skills and abilities. What can be a successful result for one person might seem mundane to another. Again, I urge you to forget what your family, friends or colleagues would think about any specific items in your list. Just write what you would consider a successful result. Don't limit yourself in this area.

It might make it easier for you to list down your 101 successes if you divide your life into about 5 or 6 periods and then write about 15 to 20 successes for each period. And after each item, write a statement to remind yourself how much of a winner and a victor you are.

Try the techniques yourself
Write down your lifetime successes

I've adopted this technique from the one I learned from Jack Canfield's coaching program.

Take stock of the nine major, breakthrough successes you've experienced in your life. Divide your life up to this point into three equal periods. For example:

Your age: 42

First third of my life: birth to age 14

Second third of my life: age 15 to 28

Third stage of my life: age 29 to present

Another example: if you're 27 years old —

First third of my life: birth to age 9

Second third of my life: age 10 to 19

Third stage of my life: age 20 to present

Then for each time period, write down the three major successes you've experienced. Don't worry if your success doesn't seem that impressive or significant by society's or the world's standards. This is your success list – what other people think doesn't matter one bit. List down what you feel is a win or a successful, victorious outcome.

Three things you did well today

Every night, before you retire, set aside 10 to 15 minutes. Take out your journal or notebook. Write down the three things you did well that day. Again, as with the above technique, it doesn't matter whether what you did well that day is small or big, major or minor. You could write, "had beautiful conversation with my daughter"; "chaired a meeting of 20 people;" "made a sale"; "signed a big client"; or "held my wife's hand as we walked".

Daily win log

It's important now to create processes that will help you be more aware of successes as they occur so that you can continue to focus on the positive and create more of it in your life.

This is a process you can begin to implement now to recognize your daily successes. You can combine this technique with any of the techniques you've learned so far in the other chapters. Combining it with the technique described in *Chapter 5 Gratitude Listing* is especially effective. Write down all your wins for the day and write down how and why you are grateful for each one of them. Do this technique mindfully. When you write your victory log, relive the feelings of victory you felt when you scored these successes. When you do appreciation writing, feel truly grateful and overjoyed at the things you appreciate in your life.

My 101 lifetime successes

Take out your journal and list down the 101 successes of your life. You might also find it easier to create a new document on your word processor and create an auto-number list with 101 numbers. This makes it easier for you to insert items or move them up or down later on. Your success list doesn't have to be chronological; it can be (like mine was) but it's not required.

Step 1: Before you start this technique, remind yourself that you are already a winner and that you are continuing to win in life. If you wish, you can write this out as a short statement and write it at the start of your list.

At the start of my list, I wrote: "These are the 101 greatest successes in my life, in no particular order. They prove that I am already a greatly successful person and that I am succeeding in life."

Step 2: Divide your life into about 5 or 6 periods and then write about 15 to 20 successes for each period. If it makes it easier, write the date or at least the year when you experienced this victory.

Step 3: After each item, write a statement to remind yourself how much of a winner and a victor you are. For example: "I am successful", "I am accomplished"; "I am distinguished"; "I can do great things"; "I am respected and accomplished".

Step 4: As you write each item, try to recall the feelings of winning and success that you felt when you scored those victories. Relish and savor the delicious feelings and sensations you felt at each of those moments. And as you do so, remind yourself of a simple truth: "I am already a winner!"

Here are some examples from my list:

> 1. All the time: hearing my mother say that I have been a dutiful son and that she is blessed to have a son like me. I am successful.

Technique Twelve: Creating solid self-confidence

14. 1989: flawlessly playing the solo guitar piece *Recuerdos dela Alhambra* before a packed theater in my high school. I am successful.

25. 1993: Scoring an A in the oral exam in one of my Philosophy classes given by a tough professor. I am distinguished.

34. 1994: After 5 years of training in Aikido, sticking to a martial art for that length of time and not quitting, being awarded my first degree blackbelt by my sensei (teacher). I am committed, self-disciplined and successful.

47. 1999: Straight out of law school, being immediately offered a job by the premier law firm in the Philippines, after a round of interviews. I later learned this was one of the fastest job offers the firm had ever made to an applicant. I am a great success.

These are just five examples. I listed down other things too that are very personal to me and that I consider big wins, like meeting Antonella for the first time and having her say yes to my invitation for a second date; paying off a huge credit card debt that I had accumulated to finance a business venture; finishing my first novel and self-publishing it.

Again, success lists are relative. Your list will surely be different from mine. List down your wins, both spectacular and humble, big and small. And as you finish your list, as you write your 101st item, know that there will be countless other victories, wins and breakthroughs waiting for you in the future. For you, this is just the beginning.

The aftermath

I am completely convinced that what separates winners – people who seem to consistently score win after win – from losers, that is, people who lose more often than they win, is that the former have utterly convinced themselves that they are winners, that if they try enough times, take enough shots, they will win. Some winners are so sure to the point perhaps of delusion that whatever it is they do, they'll win. For these people, it doesn't actually matter whether they do succeed and win each and every time; even if they fail, they still find a way to reframe that failure and consider it a win. They are fully persuaded that if they weren't 100% successful this time, then the next time they try, they will be.

> "Fine, my fifth business didn't work out. But I'm determined to be a successful business owner. I'm certain my next one will work out. And if it isn't that one, then it will be the next one."

> "Ok so this girl rejected my invitation to go on a date. That's ok, I think she's warming up to me. She'll say yes next time."

> "So the treatment for my illness didn't work. But I'll give it more time. And there are other treatments I haven't tried. One of them will work."

> "I may be up to my eye-balls in debt. But other people who were in worse situations than me were able to pay off their debts and live debt free. If they can do it, then I can too!"

> "My spouse may have walked out on me and our children. But I have faith we will be ok and we will emerge victorious in this situation."

Technique Twelve: Creating solid self-confidence

Writing down 101 reminders that I was already a winner, then reinforcing this fact everyday by writing down in my daily victory log achieved one thing for me: it elevated my level of thinking to the same level as that of the winners I've described above. It fully persuaded me that no matter how many times I fail, I have faith in myself and the next time the outcome will be different. The next shot I take, the ball will go in. The next time I swing, I'll score a home run.

Now that I've acquired this "winner's" mentality, it can't ever be taken from me. I am now living my life fully convinced that I am a winner. I am not being arrogant by believing this. I am being real.

If you develop this kind of thinking, then in time you will create unbreakable self-confidence. Your belief will be as solid as rock that no matter what life throws your way, it isn't anything you haven't dealt with before. You have won before and you will win again. Can you imagine what your life would be like if you thought this way constantly? I can imagine it. And it's the life of a victor, a conqueror, a winner.

Technique Thirteen: Charting Your Hero's Journey

Using clues from patterns of the universal human story to guide your life

In the final technique of this final chapter, I'm going to write about why you should star in your own Hollywood movie. Wait, that's not quite accurate. I'm going to write about why you are, in all likelihood, already starring in your own Hollywood movie—you just don't know it yet.

I'm here to tell you about the Hero's journey, which pervades many human stories, from Greek mythology to the modern cinema. I submit that the hero's journey resonates with many of us because the hero's journey, at its heart, is the journey we take in the course of a lifetime. I'm here to spur you to think about where you are on your hero's journey, and to share with you some valuable life lessons to be learned from this journey.

In his book, *The Hero with a Thousand Faces,* noted American mythologist Joseph Campbell talks about the hero's journey that underpins the myths and tales of almost every culture and which is still the basis of the stories we tell today. We can even find the hero's journey stamped in the storylines of Hollywood blockbusters, such as The Lord of the Rings, the Harry Potter and the Matrix series, and the original Star Wars trilogy.

This quote from Campbell's book succinctly sums up the hero's journey:

> *A hero ventures forth from the world of common day into a region of supernatural wonder. Fabulous forces are there encountered and a decisive victory is won. The hero comes back from this mysterious adventure with the power to bestow gifts on his fellow man.*

As described in this passage, the hero goes through three stages in the quest: separation, initiation and return. These are the three stages of the hero's journey. And I will show you in this chapter how these could be the stages of your own journey in life.

Think of some of the most famous stories mankind has ever told, both old and new, real or fictional, and you might see a familiar pattern.

Hercules, falls down from paradise to earth as a child, successfully performs the Twelve Labors, which involved slaying fearsome monsters, capturing fantastic beasts and collecting fabulous prizes, and later ascends to live with the gods on Mount Olympus.

Jesus Christ, Son of God, comes down from heaven and becomes man, goes out into the world to preach the good news that humanity can be saved and reunited with God, is sent to be tried and persecuted and sentenced to hang on a cross, dies, rises again after three days and ascends to heaven where he is seated at the right hand of God.

Luke Skywalker is called away from his uncle's ranch, drawn by a mysterious call for help from a princess, learns about the Force from wise mentors, confronts his greatest adversary in Darth Vader, and comes back as a fully-fledged Jedi Knight.

Technique Thirteen: Charting Your Hero's Journey

Frodo Baggins leaves the Shire with his friends, goes on a perilous quest to destroy the One Ring, battles Sauron and his orc minions, destroys the Ring in the lake of fire, and returns home, forever changed.

Simba, cub of the Lion King Mufasa, is cast out of his father's kingdom by his treacherous uncle Scar, journeys into the untamed African savannah, receives help from some animal friends, becomes a Lion King himself, and comes back to vanquish Scar and then reigns over and protects the Pride Lands.

I could give you countless other examples of heroes and heroines who have gone on their own quests, fought their own battles, conquered internal and external enemies, collected the ultimate prize, and returned home to their fellowmen to bestow gifts acquired during their journey. The pattern is similar in stories that have been told by different cultures and peoples throughout the millennia. In all these tales, we are really seeing the same Hero, who has many different faces, going on his or her own journey. This is why Campbell's book is titled *The Hero with a Thousand Faces*.

It also turns out that the enduring tales humans have told since the dawn of time all describe the same hero's journey, which in its essence, is a quest for personal transformation and self-discovery. Mythology is written for all of us; myths resonate so strongly with us because they are our stories. The authors of these mythological tales hoped that by telling them, we might see that we are all called to go on our own quests, on our own hero's journeys, and understand that all heroes go through trials and tribulations, in order to reach the end of the journey and claim whatever reward awaits us.

Thus, if we read these universal stories carefully, we can learn important clues that can teach us to recognize when we are being called to go on our own fabulous quest, what to do when we are faced with the inevitable trials and tribulations, the way to overcome them, and how to successfully complete our quests, receive the prize at the journey's end, and live the rest of our lives in peace, happiness and contentment.

Knowing all this, you will never be lost again. You will never again feel like you are going through life's challenges and trials alone. You have the template of the Hero's Journey to guide and inspire you from now on. I'll now teach you how to write your own Hero's Journey.

Recognizing the stages in the Hero's Journey

Have you ever felt like your life was one long journey? That there is a certain destination on this journey and while you might get lost from time to time, you will eventually find your way back on the right path? That you are not just a passer-by or pedestrian, but a traveller on this life? That you were called to do something special and leave your mark on this world? Or that you are being guided by forces unknown and unseen, showing you where to go and telling you what to do and providing help when you need it most?

If you have answered yes to all of the above questions, then you are not alone. Many human beings feel the same way as you. Many human beings even go so far as to acknowledge that their whole life is a hero's journey. One such person is American billionaire hedge fund manager and philanthropist Ray Dalio. In his book, *Principles,* Dalio charts his own life following the exact stages of the Hero's Journey that I've been describing above. He divided his life into the eight stages of the hero's journey:

The call to adventure

Crossing the threshold

The abyss

Technique Thirteen: Charting Your Hero's Journey

The road of trials

The ultimate boon

Returning the boon

The greatest challenge

Looking back from a higher level

So, you see, the hero's journey is not the domain only of mythical heroes or fictional adventurers. It is also the story of real-life everyday heroes such as Ray Dalio. It is not a coincidence that Dalio identified the stages of the Hero's Journey in his own life. It wasn't just his fancy to say that he went on a hero's journey just like the mythical heroes of old. He was not even saying that he was special, or some kind of hero, above the rest of us. If you step back and take stock of your own life, I believe you will see that you too are embarking or probably already going on your own hero's journey. I am convinced that you will see that you are a hero, that we are all heroes, and that we have been called to go on our own special missions in life and that we are all meant to be more, do more and live more in this life.

Let me now act as your own personal guide as we go through the stages of the hero's journey. I've adopted a streamlined version of the stages of the journey as described in Campbell's book *The Hero with a Thousand Faces*.

A short note: heroes come in all shapes, sizes, ages and genders. You and I are heroes. Men and women are heroes. For the rest of this chapter, though, I will refer to the hero in the masculine, and will sometimes use the third person pronouns "he" and "him" to replace the noun "hero". I have done this purely in the interest of brevity.

I stress, though, that whenever I refer to the "hero" in this chapter, I am always referring to you, my reader.

Stage 1: The Ordinary World

The "Ordinary World" is where the hero begins his adventure.

This is the realm of the familiar and the mundane. Here, life is comfortable, respectable but ultimately humdrum and unexciting. In the ordinary world, the hero merely exists, but does not live.

In ancient mythology, Buddha lives within the safe walls of his father's palace. In modern mythology, Frodo Baggins dwells quietly, peacefully and contentedly with his friends in the Shire. A computer programmer named Thomas Anderson, better known by his hacker alias "Neo", senses that there is something wrong with the world he lives in and is mystified by whispers of another world known as "the Matrix".

At some point in his life, the hero begins to question his everyday existence in this womb of safety, security and normalcy. For some unfathomable reason, the hero strongly feels that he doesn't quite fit in the world around him anymore. Activities and relationships that were once exciting no longer are.

"Is this all there is?" the hero wonders. The hero feels a disquieting sense of longing for something beyond the normal. The hero knows he is searching for something else, but he cannot quite put his finger on it. Whatever it is though, he knows that he will not find it in the Ordinary World he's living in.

You are the hero of this journey. At one point in your life, you may have found yourself in the Ordinary World. Something stirred within you. You are uneasy and feel disquieted about something. You know you should be content in the company of family and

Technique Thirteen: Charting Your Hero's Journey

friends; you should be satisfied with what you have. And yet you are neither contented nor satisfied.

Prepare yourself: you will very soon get a chance to step out of the Ordinary World. As you are reading this, do you feel something stirring within you?

Stage 2: Call to Adventure

Soon enough, the hero hears the Call to Adventure. As Christopher Vogler explained in his book *The Writer's Journey*, the Call may come in the form of a message or a messenger.

The Call may also simply be a feeling, a knowing that it is time for change. It almost seems like the larger world outside irresistibly beckons the hero and sends portents. These signs might come in the form of signs, dreams, visions, and strange coincidences or synchronicities.

The hero may also feel tired of being in the Ordinary World. An uncomfortable situation builds up until one final event pushes the hero to embark on an adventure.

In stories and myths, the Call comes to Moses in the form of a burning bush. It comes in God's commanding Noah to build an arc. We see the Call when Gandalf knocks on Frodo's door and warns him to leave the Shire or when Harry Potter starts receiving unsolicited letters delivered by owls.

The Call to Adventure is a wake-up call, an invitation for you to leave the Ordinary World and venture out into the unknown. When you hear the call, it feels wonderful yet scary at the same time. For the first time in your life, you are being pulled to do something outrageous that you've never done before.

The Call to Adventure is a wonderful, albeit frightening, invitation to leave the Ordinary World and journey into the unknown. It might manifest in countless ways…wanting to leave your home for a while and travel the world, feeling dissatisfied about your current job and getting excited about starting your own business or changing careers, or anything that ushers in change into your life.

Indeed, hearing the Call can be a nerve-wracking experience. But it is also an irresistible one. You might refuse the Call for a while, but you know it will come back in another shape or form. The Call invites you to cast your lot with whatever it is that awaits you beyond the Ordinary World. You know you must heed the Call sooner or later. If you don't heed the Call, you know, without a doubt, that you will be consigned to a life of regret and misery. And that is immensely more painful than whatever it is that awaits you on the other side.

Stage 3: Refusal of the Call

The hero now faces a frightening dilemma: he's being asked to heed the call to go on a journey into the great unknown that will be exciting. But it also fraught with risks and danger, and could even be life-threatening. All real adventures are. The hero agonizes over how to respond to the Call to Adventure. Those of us who have heard the Call to Adventure can relate: choosing whether or not to heed it is a most difficult choice to make. Like the hero, we find ourselves standing at the threshold of fear. It's perfectly understandable, and no one would fault us, if we momentarily hesitated or even refused to heed the Call.

The hero can't really be faulted for wanting to refuse the Call. When Christ was at the Garden of Gethsemane on the night before he was to be crucified, he asked for "this cup to pass from me". In the Matrix, after a team of agents arrived at Neo's office searching for him, he refused Morhpeus' order to jump out of a window onto a hanging scaffold because he saw it was a long drop down.

Technique Thirteen: Charting Your Hero's Journey

Christopher Vogler eloquently expressed what the hero experiences just after hearing the Call:

The specter of the unknown walks among us, halting our progress at the threshold. Some of us turn down the quest, some hesitate, some are tugged at by families who fear for our lives and don't want us to go. You hear people mutter that the journey is foolhardy, doomed from the start. You feel fear constricting your breathing and making your heart race. Should you stay with the Home Tribe, and let others risk their necks in the quest?

Most of us, at some point in our lives, were challenged to "take a leap of faith" and "jump into the unknown". These are clichéd expressions I know. But they are clichéd because they happen to be true for many people. Certainly, taking a leap of faith and jumping into the unknown might lead you to a higher, better plane of existence. But doing so could also cause you to come crashing down to the hard ground below and kill you. This is why heeding the Call is so scary: you don't know what waits on the other side.

Stage 4: Meeting with the Mentor

When the hero hears the call to adventure, he might often attempt to avoid the order. I believe this is because, whether rationally or instinctively, the hero knows that he is not ready to go on the journey. For whatever reason, he feels that he does not yet possess the knowledge, skills or experience that will be required to hurdle the obstacles that he will surely encounter on his journey. He may feel anxious about going on the journey because he knows he might not complete it unless he receives help. The hero does not feel cowardice; doubt maybe, as to whether he's cut out for this adventure. But he never feels cowardice.

Vogler explains that it might not be a bad idea for the hero to refuse the Call until he has had time to prepare for the unknown that waits for him. We've seen this in tales and myths. In Genesis, Moses heard the Call to Adventure when God asked him to go before the Pharaoh and demand that he let the Israelites go free. Moses gave so many excuses to God – I'm not good enough, I don't have all the answers, people won't believe me, I'm a terrible public speaker, I'm not qualified. Sounds familiar? They are the same excuses that many heroes, yes, I'm referring to you, have given at one point or another to justify refusing to heed the Call.

When the hero is most doubtful, even most fearful, about whether he should heed the Call, it is exactly at this point that he should heed it and commit to going on the adventure. It is because it is at this point, as our most enduring stories, both mythical and real, tell us, when help will arrive. Enter the Mentor.

When the hero listens to the Call and accepts the challenge of going on the quest, he always receives help, sometimes from the most unexpected sources. In *The Karate Kid*, when Daniel was ready, Miyagi appears just in time to teach him Karate. In *The Lion King*, Simba has Pumbaa and Timon. Luke had Obi-Wan, Han Solo and Yoda, and Harry had Ron, Hermione and Dumbledore.

In real life, help has often come to heroes in the form of mentors and friends. It might be a chance meeting with the mentor, who comes in the form of a teacher or coach offering exactly what the hero needs to be successful.

How many times were you hesitating about doing something you've dreamed of doing for the longest time when you suddenly receive unexpected help that finally allows you to undertake this task? Sometimes the help might not even come from a person but from an object like a book or a piece of conversation that you hear from someone. No matter the form that the mentor takes, he or she

Technique Thirteen: Charting Your Hero's Journey

will give you the skills, knowledge and confidence that you need to overcome your fear and commence the adventure.

As you might have already realized, you cannot complete the journey on your own. If you've already accepted the Call and feel that you have not yet found your mentors, just be patient and look harder. I assure you that they are there. You just might not recognize the form they have taken.

Stage 5: Crossing the first threshold

Blessed with Supernatural Aid, the Hero leaves the Ordinary World and embarks on an adventure. But he must do one thing first before fully embracing the quest: he must cross the first threshold.

We see the heroes' crossing of the threshold as Frodo and Sam step out of the Shire and the latter says: "This is it. If I take one more step, it'll be the farthest away from home I've even been." We again see it happen when the Fellowship of the Ring passes through the Argonath, two monolithic pillars shaped as kings of old, a literal threshold that leads on to greater and more dangerous adventures.

At this point, the hero has already heeded the call, confronted his doubts and allayed his fears. He has the mentor's wisdom to help guide and prepare him for the adventure that awaits. Now the hero stands at the entrance of this new world of adventure.

All he has to do is walk through it.

This is not the easiest thing in the world to do. It takes a strong act of will for the hero to walk through the threshold and wholeheartedly commit himself to the quest. It's exhilarating yet frightening all at once. And the hero knows that once he overcomes his fear and crosses the threshold, there is no going back.

In tales and myths, Alice falls down the rabbit hole into Wonderland, Neo accepts Morpheus' invitation to take the red pill and gets his eyes opened to the Matrix.

In real life, some of you might have crossed the threshold of the world of adventure when you moved out of your parents' house into the big, wide world, or sold your possessions, quit your job and bought a one-way ticket to somewhere. Like the mythological heroes, you know you have committed to the journey and whatever happens, you cannot go back to the word you left behind.

This can be a humbling and painful experience. It doesn't always lead to a romantic and fantastic world the hero imagined. It doesn't always immediately lead to a wonderful adventure. Some heroes who have stepped through the threshold have found themselves thrust into life and death situations straight away – just ask Jonah when he found himself in the belly of a whale. When we go through all the stages of the hero's journey up to this point and seemingly do everything right, and end up being stuck in the "belly of the whale", we might experience some remorse, even regret. What on earth were we thinking! We were perfectly content in the Ordinary World and we had to go out on this silly quest, now look where we've ended up?

Regardless of the form it takes, the threshold is fiendishly difficult to cross. But eventually the hero crosses the threshold and somehow survives the experience.

Stage 6: The Road of Trials

Now that hero has completely entered into the fullness of adventure, which Joseph Campbell described as "a dream landscape of curiously fluid, ambiguous forms", he goes through a series of trials. Perhaps the hero intuitively knows that the going won't be easy once he goes on his quest, and he is utterly unprepared to deal with the trials when they do come.

Before Hercules became a true hero, he needed to execute the 12 labors. Before Maximus the Gladiator found Elysium, he had to fight in the Colosseum.

Technique Thirteen: Charting Your Hero's Journey

Facing these trials is a truly frightening experience for all heroes. The hero doesn't know if he has what it takes to overcome these trials.

In a similar vein, you must overcome your own challenges and successfully navigate your own road of trials if you want to become the best and strongest version of yourself. As a blade is tempered by the intense heat from a furnace, and as coal must be subjected to unimaginable pressures for eons to become a diamond, so too must you be tested. This is life's way of tempering you, to see if you can withstand the heat and pressure needed for transformation.

Stage 7: Final Ordeal

Eventually, the hero must face the biggest monster alone. Before Siddhartha Gautama became Buddha, and before Jesus Christ went on his mission to save humankind, they had to endure temptations. In myths and stories, Luke Skywalker had to enter the cave and face his deepest fear. Harry Potter had to duel Voldemort. Gladiator Maximus had to battle Commodus in the Colosseum. Every hero who has made it this far has had to face and slay their own demons and dragons.

By no stretch of the imagination is it easy to do this. Most real life, everyday heroes, when faced by their enemy, are quite understandably tempted to give up and surrender. The sirens' song of a carefree, easy and comfortable life beckons. It seems easier to capitulate.

Take an athlete who dreams of achieving greatness and reaching the pinnacle of her sport. Before she realizes her goals, she is faced with the mammoth task of developing all skills needed to win, and she must practice and repeat the same movements thousands of times until they become second nature to her. Through this process, she comes to know the true meaning of sacrifice.

This does not mean that that athlete is not tempted to quit. If you study the lives of great athletes, at many points in their careers, they almost gave up prematurely, before they reached greatness.

In your own journeys, you may have been battered and bruised after going through the gauntlet of ordeals and trials. You may have been tempted to give up and surrender, and to settle down and rest. But you always knew, on a visceral level, that you had to face this final ordeal and overcome it.

Stage 8: The Ultimate Prize

The hero ultimately faces the dragon. The fear that the hero feels is beyond anything he's ever felt before. Faced with the impossible task of slaying the dragon, the hero suddenly feels so insignificant. The hero is wounded. His ultimate defeat now seems a foregone conclusion.

Faced with the prospect of his imminent destruction, all his resources exhausted, the hero surrenders. Not to the enemy but to his fate. He does not capitulate, nor does he resign himself to defeat. Instead, he yells out to the enemy, "go ahead, do your worst! You may defeat me, but you will never conquer me!" With these words, the hero ceases to struggle and allows nature to take its course.

In myths and tales, it is this act of surrender that transforms the hero. One aspect of the hero may die or be destroyed as a result of the final ordeal. Paradoxically, in suffering ultimate defeat, the hero wins. For what emerges from this final ordeal is the hero transformed. The hero is perfected by this experience. This is the ultimate prize of victory.

We see it happen in the most revered tales. Hercules becomes a god. Christ dies on the cross but is resurrected and ascends to heaven. Siddhartha Gautama achieves enlightenment and becomes Buddha. In more familiar stories, Luke Skywalker becomes a Jedi

Knight, and Neo fully embraces his identity as "the One". It is the same for all mythological or fictional heroes.

In life, often our greatest defeats precede our greatest victories. This experience too is the same for all real-life heroes.

Stage 9: The Road Back

The hero wins the ultimate prize. He gains the ultimate boon. He obtains the Holy Grail. He becomes one with The Force. The hero's journey, however, does not end here. The hero still has to return home.

Just as heeding the call to adventure was difficult, so is the call to return. The hero initially did not even want to go on this journey but wanted to stay within the familiar confines of his home. But now he has completed the journey, ironically, the hero is reluctant to travel back.

After almost losing his life to destroy Sauron's ring, Frodo doesn't want to leave the tranquillity of Rivendell and return home to the Shire. He can hardly be blamed for wanting to stay. When the hero has tasted paradise, when he has known what it's like to live with the ultimate prize, going back to his old, imperfect and mundane life is not appealing. Yet the hero knows, as all true heroes do, that he cannot stay in paradise. He is needed by those he has left behind. To stay and deprive them of experiencing the ultimate prize he has won would be selfish. He knows he must return home.

The return to the ordinary world of imperfection, of pain and suffering is the final act of redemption for the hero. Moses came down from Mount Sinai with the ten commandments. Jesus, Buddha, Muhammad and all the prophets of old came back to the world of humans to share their wisdom and spread their message.

After overcoming their greatest struggle and winning the ultimate prize, everyday heroes feel an obligation to give back of the wisdom and share their experience to help others who are about to go on their own adventures.

Stage 10: Looking back from a higher level

So ends the Hero's journey. The hero can now rest, but not for long. For the hero's journey never truly ends. As soon as one journey is completed, the hero soon hears a familiar call. It's the call to embark on another adventure. There are new goals to be set, new challenges to be overcome. Another mountain waits to be climbed, another race calls to be run, another channel beckons to be swum. It has been this way in myths and stories. This is also why we have movie sequels!

We are, each of the us, the mythical hero and the hero's journey is our story. And just as the hero's' journey in myths and tales never ends, our own journey of life also never really ends. As long as we are living and breathing and walking this earth, we continue to go on our own quests and write our own stories. After we have overcome our own road of trials, conquered our final ordeals and returned with the ultimate prize, it's now time to use the lessons we have learned as we continue our journeys. We get to relish the ultimate prize in whatever form it came to us – as knowledge, wisdom, fame, fortune, love or simply just the experience of a lifetime – and also to share it with the world if we choose.

Now it's time for you, the hero, to rest. But don't rest too long though. For now, something is calling you. Listen closely and you will hear the beating of your heart. It's growing louder and louder because it feels the thrill of a new adventure coming. It's time to start another hero's journey.

Technique Thirteen: Charting Your Hero's Journey

Try it yourself: charting your own Hero's Journey

Why is it important to chart your own hero's journey? How will it help you if you could identify each stage of the hero's journey as you step into it?

I believe it's important because knowing you are traversing your own hero's journey can show you that your life is not an aimless wander through planet Earth; it can show you that the events in your life are not just a series of random occurrences that were decided by a cosmic roll of the dice. Knowing that your life is a journey can have profound impact for you because you know that you are meant to go somewhere in your life, to do something worthwhile and valuable with your stay here on this planet. It strengthens your faith that your existence has a purpose and that you were put here to play a unique part in the grand human story, in the opera of life.

Recognizing that you are not alone as you struggle through the various trials, tests and tribulations life brings you, and that others who are in the middle of their own hero's journeys are experiencing the same things, will encourage you and keep you from capitulating to life's challenges. It will push you to stay on course amidst these challenges because you know that supernatural aid is assured for all those who persevere.

Knowing that you are connected with the rest of humanity – the countless ones who have come before you, the ones who are now living and the others who will come – and that all our stories are made up of the same threads of one story, the hero's journey, will forever shatter any sense of isolation or parochialism you might have.

Finally, being aware that you are embarking on your own hero's journey gives you an inner GPS, an infallible guiding system that you can always rely on to bring you back on the right path when you feel you've lost your way.

Now let's try charting your hero's journey. For this exercise, I've adopted the stages of Joseph Campbell's hero's journey. I have, however, slightly modified the hero's journey by making its stages more concise and compacting it into its most essential elements.

Divide your life into roughly the eight stages listed below. Depending on how young or old you are, I suspect that not all of these stages will be applicable to you. My older readers may find that they've lived through all of these stages, or perhaps even already completed several cycles of the hero's journey. If this true of you, then I celebrate you as person and as a hero. Your stories of challenge and triumph are worth telling the world. The world has much to benefit from your knowledge and wisdom.

On the other hand, my younger readers may find that they are just now hearing the call to adventure or have only taken their first tentative steps out of the ordinary world and through the first threshold into the unknown world. If this applies to you, then I congratulate you for being courageous enough to heed the call to adventure and embark on your hero's journey. You're about to get the experience of a lifetime!

Here are the 10 stages of your hero's journey:

Stage 1: The Ordinary World

Stage 2: My Call to Adventure

Stage 3: Meeting my Mentors

Stage 4: Crossing the first threshold

Stage 5: My Road of Trials

Stage 6: The Dragon's Den

Stage 7: My moment of despair

Stage 8: Attaining the Ultimate Prize

Technique Thirteen: Charting Your Hero's Journey

Stage 9: Returning with the Prize

Stage 10: Looking back from a higher level

You'll note that I have used the first person pronoun "my" in the headings of most of the stages. This is because person I'm referring to in each stage is *you*. These are stages of your own hero's journey.

The hero's journey will run the course of your entire lifetime. For that reason, applying this technique doesn't have any deadline or time limit. It's something that you can work on for years; but it can also be something that you do in a single day, as you retreat from the busy, workaday world and take stock of where your life is going.

Think about the questions associated with each stage of the hero's journey and write your answers in your journal. If you come to other realizations as you reflect on each stage, then write those down too.

Stage 1: The Ordinary World

Before I can enter a higher level of life, I must first live in the ordinary world. Apart from my actual environment, the ordinary world can also represent my comfort zone, conditioned beliefs and behaviors.

- What does the ordinary world look like for me?
- What is my current comfort zone?
- Do I feel like I'm going through my current life in a daze, like I am just going through the motions of living?
- Am I living my life bored, listless, without any passion or excitement?

Stage 2: My Call to Adventure

The Call to Adventure is a call for me to leave the ordinary world and travel to a special one, a world in which I will be actualizing all my potential as a person, and using my gifts and talents to become the best version of myself and serve humanity and the world.

- Do I feel an urge to do something out of the ordinary in my life? In my work? In my relationships? In my living arrangements?
- Do I sense that I need to change something in my life or the way I've been living it?
- Is there something I know I must do that will serve my highest good as a person, but which I am resisting?
- Is there an important decision that could potentially change my life (and by extension my family's life) for the better, which I am afraid to make or am putting off?
- Do I feel the need to get out of my comfort zone and venture into an unknown, but exciting, future?
- Do I have a grand vision for my life, in which I am existing as the best possible version of myself, in which the different areas of my life have reached their highest levels?
- Is there something that my heart is pulling me to do but which my brain is discouraging me from doing because it's unrealistic, impractical or will never work?

Stage 3: Meeting my Mentors

At one point in my quest, someone unexpectedly comes along offering me aid, assistance or encouragement that could help me travel farther or overcome the challenges and obstacles blocking my path. I don't know when the mentor will appear but I have faith that he or she will come when I am ready.

- Are there any people in my life right now who know the mission I've decided to take and are already helping me in some way to succeed in it?
- Am I accepting or refusing their offer of aid?
- Who are the people whose help, knowledge, wisdom, talents, skills or resources I will need to help me achieve my goals?
- If a potential mentor is present, what actions can I take to get them to know and help me?
- Can I seek help, wisdom or advice from my higher self or inner guidance system?

Stage 4: Crossing the First Threshold

Once I go through the first door or cross the first bridge, it bursts into flames. I cannot turn back, at least not the way by which I came.

- What major decision can I make right now that would represent the first step out of my comfort zone and toward my envisioned life?
- What one powerful action can I take right now that would show that I am committed to moving toward my big goals?
- What one act am I afraid or even terrified of doing but which I know, if I did it, will represent a breakthrough in my life and in my goals?

Stage 5: My Road of Trials

Along my hero's journey, I expect to encounter many obstacles and challenges. I anticipate facing many foes, whether human, material, situational or circumstantial, all intent on stopping me from completing my journey and finding my treasure. This comes as no surprise. I expect this because I acknowledge that adversity is how the universe tests my commitment to succeed in my journey.

- What obstacles lie between me and the higher vision I have seen for my life?

- What challenges are hindering me from taking further steps toward my goals?

- Are there people who are trying to stop me from moving forward in my quest?

- Are there any circumstances, situations, conditions or factors that are making it difficult for me to continue moving toward my goals?

Stage 6: The Dragon's Den

The next threshold is often more challenging or treacherous than the first. This could involve a second major decision that I take along my hero's journey; it could put me at significant physical and psychological risk. But I also realize that within the walls of my darkest, innermost cave also lies the cornerstone of the special world I am trying to reach. I know that my goal is within reach.

- Are there signs that my goal or objective is now coming closer to me?

Technique Thirteen: Charting Your Hero's Journey

- Do things feel more difficult now that I can see my goal?

- What challenges or obstacles am I facing right now that are hindering me from achieving my ultimate objective?

- Am I tempted to give in to despair and lose hope, abandon my quest and give up?

Stage 7: My Moment of Despair

I know that the journey toward my ultimate goal is an adventure. And no adventure worth taking is ever easy. I realize that there are many dangers that lie before me on the path to self-realization and self-discovery. I must not give up and lose hope, knowing that success is assured as long as I persevere toward my ultimate goal.

- Does it seem like nothing is happening and that I'm not getting any closer to my goal or objective?

- Am I now doubting that I can succeed in my quest and achieve my ultimate goal?

- Am I faced with a major obstacle that is making my immediate future look dark?

- Does it look like I'm stuck in a trap, that mentally I cannot see a way ahead, and that I'm about to lose my way, my self or my values in my quest toward my goal?

- Can I draw on resources, both internal (my hidden reserves of energy, strength, faith, industry and creativity) and external (other people, my own support networks), to help me survive this ordeal and successfully emerge from the cave?

Stage 8: Attaining the Ultimate Prize

I have now overcome my major obstacles and emerged from my dark cave of doubt and despair. I have successfully achieved my ultimate goal. I have attained my desire. I have reached the end of my journey and arrived at my destination. While I may have obtained the prize, I realize that the real reward is my own inner transformation.

- How have I changed as a person by having completed my quest and achieved my goals?

- What are the valuable lessons I have learned during this process?

- Do I feel an obligation to share what I have learned with others, to help them on their own hero's journey?

- What am I impelled to do now that I have been successful in my quest?

Stage 9: Returning with the Prize

I acknowledge that my entire life is one big adventure, an unending quest to realize my highest self and be the best version of myself. There will always be challenges ahead of me, both physical, psychological, mental and even spiritual. I am determined to overcome all these challenges. I also recognize that there will be future calls to adventure and further journeys for me to embark on.

- What new challenges or roadblocks still lie in front of me as I make my way back after achieving my goal?

- After I have completed my hero's journey, are there any unresolved issues that I must now face and resolve?

- After gaining valuable lessons from my quest, am I being called to share my newfound knowledge to serve humanity and the world?

- Can I identify personal areas of weakness that I must improve if I am to become the best possible version of myself?

Stage 10: Looking back from a higher level

Before coming home with my new-found wisdom, there is often one more unforeseen challenge. This trial could be the most difficult of them all; it is a test that I must pass to cement my personal transformation.

- What unsuspected ordeal has now emerged after I have achieved my ultimate goal?

- What new knowledge and skills have I gained from my quest that I can now use to overcome this final hurdle?

- Do I feel more confident that I am able to handle the demands brought about by my new life?

Key points to remember

While each of our hero's journeys is unique, there will still be stages similar from one person's journey to another. Although each of our stories is special and different from any other person's story, still our stories have common threads, elements drawn from the universal human story that we all have a hand in writing.

You may find that you survive your moment of despair and emerge from your dragon's lair unsuccessful in your quest and without the prize you originally set out to attain. Do not let this discourage you from continuing to realize your highest potential and becoming the best possible version of yourself. This is not the final chapter of your story. Far from it. It's only the beginning. There will be other opportunities to go on the hero's journey.

You will hear the Call to Adventure again soon enough. This is how the universe seems to work. You will be given a chance to go on a similar adventure as the one you just took. If you do not heed this call to adventure, another one will come. If you do listen to it and embark on a new adventure, you will continue to be tested until you succeed and learn the lessons you're meant to learn or you give up.

But you will not give up because you know deep inside that you will win as long as you don't quit. If the experiences of countless humans who have gone on the hero's journey are anything to go by, you know that if you are committed to completing your own journey and grabbing the prize that lies waiting at the end of the path, then the universe will conspire to help you succeed.

At the start, your hero's journey is about accomplishment. You might be attempting to build a business while you're working in a job, get fit, raise a family, travel to a faraway land, or become the best you can possibly be at your craft, discipline or profession. All these are worthwhile goals that often spur you toward your hero's journey. Certainly, you will want to claim the big prize that awaits you at the end of your quest. Only you can say what that ultimate prize is – knowledge, wisdom, experience, fame, fortune, love or simply the adventure of a lifetime.

Along the way, however, if you pay attention, you will clearly realize that the big prize you were after has become only secondary; what's more valuable are the lessons you're learning, learnings that are slowly transforming you into the best possible version of yourself that you can be.

Part Three:

Troubleshooting and FAQs

Technique Thirteen: Charting Your Hero's Journey

What do I do if I've written everything down and nothing happened?

Pause for a moment and think. Perhaps it did happen, but not in the way you were expecting. Go back through your writing. You may have written the core reason why you wanted this outcome in the first place. You might have already found what you sought or received what you asked for, but it came from a different channel or in another form.

The universe is infinitely capable of giving you what you earnestly desire; but there are times when the universe does not give you what you want, but what you need, what's meant for your highest end. Think about the times in your life when you really wished for something (or someone) and you did not get what you wanted. Later on, you realize that had you actually gotten what you originally asked for, things might not have worked out for the best or getting what you wanted might have ended up harming you.

It's also possible that what you wrote about did happen, but it happened long after the timeframe you intended and you forgot that you once actually wrote about it. Look back, review your writing and you might be astounded that something that you wrote about years ago and have now forgotten has actually come to pass.

I've written about the perfect outcome I desired and I briefly got what I wanted. But then, everything fell apart. Did I fail?

A breakdown often presages realignment and reordering. You've gotten very clear about what you want in life, the types of people you want to be surrounded with, and the quality of experiences you wish to experience. You've written it all down. Through your writing, you've drawn a line in the sand that no matter what happens from this point on, you are moving ahead and achieving your vision.

Then, unexpectedly, you experience a setback: you lose a key customer, get fired from a job, experience a relationship breakup or receive a bad medical report. Believe it or not, this could be good for you. When it looks like things are breaking down, you can expect that everything is about to be set right. Disorder and chaos are often necessary prior to completion.

We see this cycle everywhere – in nature, commerce, relationships, and many other areas. Learn to recognize this cycle; when you do, you will start to have a different attitude toward breakdowns. You will not be distressed or anxious. Instead, you can rejoice knowing that you are getting closer to accomplishing your goal, finding what you seek, and realizing what you've envisioned.

How long does it take before I see results from my writing?

I've discussed the subject of timing in almost all of the techniques described in this book. In truth, this question has so many layers that one page is not nearly enough to adequately answer it.

I can, however, share some observations. In my experience, when I write things down, they materialize faster in direct proportion to the level of my unbiased and unquestioning expectation. When I am absolutely convinced that the outcome I want is the next logical step, when I am so sure that it's going to happen that I am no longer too excited or giddy about it, when I take on an easy attitude of "oh for sure it's going to happen now", that's when results seem to happen faster. An attitude of surrender has a lot to do with this.

Technique Thirteen: Charting Your Hero's Journey

When I've done everything I can to achieve a specific outcome, including writing about it, I reach a point of peace. A stillness comes over me knowing that my part of the work is done and it's now up to the unseen forces around me to orchestrate people, things, events and circumstances to deliver to me what I want. A quiet confidence overcomes me that what I seek is now on its way, naturally, easily, logically, without any further need for intervention on my part.

It is always at this point when what I've desired shows itself in my experience.

Yes, I wrote about what I want, and wrote and wrote some more. But nothing seems to be changing in my circumstances. What do I do?

Go back Chapter 7 and re-read Nadia's story. Her deepest desire at one point in her life was to find an emotionally, financially, professionally, and psychologically fulfilling job in her field. For more than four years, during which she wrote about getting this dream job, nothing seemed to happen. In fact, the very opposite of nothing happening was happening – she was getting rejected left and right by prospective employers. It was when she let go of her desire, when she stopped holding on to it that it started coming toward her.

Remember, the time when you think nothing is happening is really when things are happening. You just don't see it. This is evident in nature. You don't see the seed in the process of sprouting from the ground; one moment it's invisible under the ground, and the next, a sapling has burst forth. You don't actually see a flower growing but you know it is. At low tide, when the land is exposed, you know, without seeing any direct evidence, that soon the tides will come and cover the land.

When you've written it down and taken actions that are within your control, trust that things will now happen, things that you cannot see. Have faith that things are being orchestrated for your good. The Bible described it beautifully and accurately: "Now faith is the substance of things hoped for, the evidence of things not seen." There will come a point when you will know with certainty it's right to stop writing for the moment and *surrender*. That word does not mean resigning to a state of affairs, but to stop resisting the seeming inactivity around you. When you surrender, that's when you free things to flow to bring about the conditions and circumstances you desire.

I know some successful people and high achievers who have never written anything down on paper. Is it really necessary that I write something down before I can get or achieve it?

What's the difference between someone who wishes or fantasizes about something, and somebody who imagines things?

It's intention and commitment. It's one thing to dream about building a bridge but it's a totally different thing to imagine how to build it. The engineer imagines the design for the bridge, how the bridge will be built, with the intention of actually building it. Things come into being not by being wished, but by being imagined and acted upon.

As Henriette Klauser explained in *Write It Down, Make It Happen*, when we fantasize, there is no commitment to creating it; but when we imagine something with a personal commitment, then it happens. Intention and commitment are the keys. What writing does is to get us out of fantasizing and dreaming and to elevate us to the level of commitment.

Technique Thirteen: Charting Your Hero's Journey

I have always found that committing things to paper has a clarifying and galvanizing effect. Writing an intention or a plan down brings certainty and solidity to my intentions.

As I explained in the foreword, there are many important reasons why we write, why we should write. And writing to achieve something is only one of the reasons for doing it. Scientific and academic research has repeatedly proven that writing down things by hand brings many benefits. This was explained by Sarah Harvey in an article written in CNBC.com on 'Kakeibo', the amazingly effective Japanese art of personal finance which employs only a pen and paper. Writing can help us make positive changes by encouraging us to be more present and aware. It can also help us identify the triggers for negative habits.

It's true that not a lot of people write. But with the help of this book, you will discover the power that lies waiting to be tapped when you write. And when you do, you'll wonder why you waited this long to start writing.

Ok so I've written stuff down and followed all instructions in this book. Do I have to do anything else?

If, in the process of your writing, you are prompted to do a specific action or take a step in a certain direction, then do it. You will find that this is inspired action, the kind of action that brings genuine results.

Sometimes, however, after you write, the next action that you are prompted to do is to do nothing, to sit and be still. The Book of Ecclesiastes reminds us that "there is a time for everything, and a season for every activity under the heavens". There is "a time to embrace and a time to refrain from embracing, a time to search and a time to surrender".

There is also a difference between active and passive waiting. Active waiting involves waiting with a spirit of expectation that what we want is on its way to us. Passive waiting is merely passing the time without any expectation or even hope that anything will happen. While actively waiting, it's also a good idea to give thanks in advance. Thanking God before you receive an answer to your prayer is one of the highest forms of prayer. It shows faith and confidence that you are a child of God and that he will give you what you ask for if you only have faith that you will receive it. Jesus said in the Gospel of Saint Mark, "all things are possible for one who believes". Let's take him at his word and believe!

If you feel you really need to do something, then write about it. Clarify the reasons why you think doing a certain act or taking a specific step will be beneficial for your cause.

Do I need to believe in a higher power – God, Allah, Buddha, the Universe, Infinite Intelligence, etc, – for my writing to work?

My personal belief is that writing is one of those ways (the other ways being prayer and meditation) that are given to us human beings to directly connect with higher power, or the higher forces surrounding us. Whatever or however you regard this higher power or these higher forces to be is something purely personal to you.

Whether you believe in God, Allah, Buddha, the Universe or Infinite Intelligence, ultimately it doesn't matter. What matters is that by writing, you are demonstrating a firm belief that you are not alone in your search or quest and that you're relying on someone for guidance and assistance along the way.

If you don't believe in the aforementioned entities, then believe in yourself. You – your *unconscious mind* as described by Joseph Murphy, or *the other self* according to Napoleon Hill – are the higher power. Believe in your own mind, your own innate intelligence and creativity to figure out solutions to problems that life throws at you, your own industriousness to imagine ways of achieving your goals, and your own determination to carry out your plans.

What's more powerful – writing something down or speaking it?

I see writing and speaking as two halves of the one gift given to humans by the divine. Often the latter follows naturally from the former. When I've written about a desire, goal or outcome that really matters to me, I often find myself moved to share what I've written with others. It could be with my partner or business associates. I share it with them to inspire them, get their feedback or get them on board with my vision. And because I've written it down, it makes it easier for me to share it with them.

Some of the techniques in WriteTech, for instance, Writing to the 100th Power (technique two) and Gratitude Listing (technique five) might involve you writing the same things every day. Writing the same things daily can be done partly as an act of affirmation or meditation. It can also be done to focus our minds and attention, as well as imprint things in our unconscious minds.

As Henriette Klauser explained, a vividly imagined image with emotional content is as strong as an actual experience as far as the brain and the 'other-than-conscious' mind (her term for the inner or unconscious mind) are concerned. By repeatedly writing things, you feed your inner mind and provide the universe with living descriptions of the things, outcomes and experiences you want of this world. This is another reason to write the same things every day.

You might have many other questions that are not included above. I've limited the questions to eight. This is deliberate. I am hoping that you will welcome new questions that come to mind as you go through the techniques and allow yourselves the opportunity to discover the answers on your own. As with anything in WriteTech, the answers to many of our questions are uncovered through our writing.

If you have any questions or stories to share, please drop me a line at ***Jonathan@writetech.co***

Appendices

The techniques of WriteTech at a glance

The following pages contain a summary of each WriteTech technique—categorized according to its purpose, with instructions on when to use it and how to apply the technique.

Blank writing sheets that you can use or adopt to practice each of these techniques are available to download for free: visit ***www.writetech.co.***

Use these as templates and experience the power of each technique.

WRITING TO CO-CREATE

Writing to the 100th Power (technique 2)

When to use: to intensify the effects of your writing to achieve a specific outcome within a deadline.

Instructions:

Step 1: Get your journal or notebook.

Step 2: Choose a time most suitable for writing undisturbed for about 15 minutes to half an hour.

Step 3: Write down the single, all important goal you want to achieve.

Step 4: Describe the goal in detail.

- Ask: what is the first thing I would do right after I achieve this goal?
- Ask: what is the last step to happen that would imply, without a doubt, that my goal has been achieved?

As you write about the act you would immediately do right after you achieved your goal, be sure to include and describe the feelings you would be experiencing.

Step 5: Feel yourself actually experiencing these feelings at the present moment. Write about it.

Step 6: Indicate the day on which you are writing. Example: write that in 100, or 89 or 57 or 28 days, etc, your desired outcome will come to pass or you will achieve your goal.

Life Scripting (technique 3)

When to use: to write out your life script; to design and plan in advance your ideal future life.

Instructions:

Twenty things you enjoy doing

Use this technique to discover your personal style.

Step 1: Draw a chart, with two columns—a left-hand side vertical column, and a right-hand side horizontal column.

Step 2: On the vertical column, list down the 20 things; there's no need to rank them; it will be impossible to rank them anyway because these are all things you enjoy.

Step 3: On the horizontal column, write the questions below. You might have to turn your paper landscape style to fit these.

Q1: How long since last done?

Q2: Costs money or free?

Q3: Alone or with someone?

Q4: Planned or spontaneous?

Q5: Work or family related?

Q6: Physical risk?

Q7: What do I like about it?

Q8: Involves mind, body or spirit?

Step 4: Write down your answers to each question.

Step 5: Analyze your answers.

Step 6: Write down what you discover about yourself.

Life scripting 1—designing your ideal environment

Step 1: Suspend your judgment.

Step 2: Answer this question: in what imaginary environment would my best self emerge?

Step 3: Imagine your ideal environment: an environment that is perfect for someone with all your present characteristics.

Step 4: Write down your answers.

Step 5: List some adjectives describing what positive qualities in you would emerge if you were in that environment.

Step 6: Analyze your ideal environment.

Step 7: Write down what you discover about yourself.

Life scripting 2—describing your perfect day

Step 1: Now that you know the 20 things you enjoy doing and your perfect environment, answer these questions:

- how would you spend your time?
- who would you spend it with?
- what sorts of things would you be doing?

Step 2: Write your answer. Describe events visually and sequentially.

Step 3: Analyze your perfect day.

Step 4: Write down what you discover about yourself.

GoalSeek (technique 4)

When to use: to identify and choose your true, overriding goals, write and prioritize them, and start an action plan.

Instructions:

GoalSeek

Touchstone method

Step 1: Take any goal you want, the bigger the better. Write down that goal in your journal.

Step 2: Subject it to the "SWSWSW…Next!" process: keep asking why you want this goal and write down your answers; keep asking and writing until you reach the touchstone goal. This goal becomes your first target.

Step 3: On a fresh page, write down the touchstone goal and underline it. Then list down every way you can think of that could possibly bring you that touchstone.

Step 4: Rank each way you come up with in terms of what's most doable right now.

Bite-sizing method

Step 1: Go through the description that you wrote of your ideal day.

Step 2: Among the elements of that ideal day, which ones are indispensable, the highest-priority items that are absent from your life at this moment? Write those elements down. These become your first targets.

Step 3: Among these elements you listed, which one can you get in the cheapest, easiest and fastest way possible? This becomes square one, your starting point.

GoalList

Step 1: Compose your own list of goals. Use the 5 criteria listed for a true, overriding goal.

Step 2: Write fast. Do not linger over the page.

Step 3: Time-stamp each goal. Set a deadline for the achievement of each goal and write down that goal in the present tense as if it has already been achieved, and inject verbs or active descriptors of what you're feeling.

Step 4: After listing each goal, write down at least one definite and concrete action that you can take now toward that goal.

Love letters to and from a future beloved (technique 11)

When to use: to attract a perfect mate or life partner or ideal relationship.

Instructions:

Step 1: Write a detailed description of what you want in an ideal relationship, mate or partner.

Step 2: Be as specific as you want in your description. Write your answers to these questions:

- what would your everyday be like if you are already living your dream relationship with your ideal partner or mate?

- how do you feel now that your ideal partner or mate is now in your life?

Step 3: Write a letter to him or her. Write as many letters as you feel like writing.

Step 4: If you feel things are taking too long and you are feeling doubtful, impatient or desperate, ask these questions and write down your answers:

- what lessons do I need to learn from this experience of waiting?
- what do I need to do to perfect myself during this period of necessary waiting?

WRITING TO RECEIVE ANSWERS

Mind Your Energy (technique 1)

When to use: to control your mental focus, direct your will power, and manage your internal states; to avoid the state of 'overwhelm' when faced with a problem.

Instructions:

Step 1: Do first thing in the morning or just prior to sleep.

Step 2: Be in a relaxed state and environment.

Step 3: Pull a problem out of your life, something that's a real tough challenge right now.

Step 4: Ask yourself each of the 5 powerful questions in turn, out loud:

1) What's great about this? or What's good about this? (If your brain says, "nothing" then ask "What could be great about this?")

2) What's not perfect yet? (presupposing it's going to be perfect)

3) What am I willing to do to make it the way I want it?

4) What am I willing to no longer do in order to make things the way I want them?

5) How can I do what's necessary to get this job done and enjoy the process?

Step 5: Wait for answers.

Step 6: Write down the answers as they come.

Superconscious Writing (technique 6)

When to use: to tap into higher intelligence when needing to come up with brilliant, ground-breaking ideas; when looking for an answer to a question, guidance or inspiration.

Instructions:

Remember this key: the Superconscious Mind is activated by clear, specific and written goals, intensely desired, visualized regularly, and constantly worked toward.

How to tap into the Superconscious Mind

Writing in white heat

Step 1: Relax, calm and center yourself.

Step 2: Be ready to write.

Step 3: Set a time limit.

Step 4: Pose a specific question to or make a specific request of the Superconscious Mind.

Step 5: Write in white heat. During the allotted time, write non-stop every single idea and detail that comes to you.

Step 6: Leave it alone.

Evening and Morning pages

This technique can be used on its own or in conjunction with writing in white heat.

Step 1: Set your alarm clock for the next morning, 15-20 minutes before you ordinarily rise.

Step 2: Bring a pad or notebook and pen right into bed with you or put them on your beside table, so you're ready to write once you awake.

Step 3: About 15 minutes before you go to bed, meditate on the question you want to ask or a request you want to address the Superconscious Mind.

Step 4: Write down the question or request on paper. Ask plenty of questions connected with what you're trying to accomplish and note them on paper.

Step 5: Keep writing until you're ready to fall asleep. If nothing comes, don't stress.

Step 6: As soon as you wake up the next morning, start writing on your pad or notebook.

Step 7: Do "warm-up" writing. Write sleepy, twilight-zone thoughts or any thoughts that come to mind.

Step 8: Write down the impressions you get relating to your questions or requests from the previous evening. If you had any dreams, write them down with as much detail as possible. Keep writing until the allotted time is over.

Step 9: Repeat steps 1 to 8 faithfully over the next several days (two weeks are recommended) without re-reading what you wrote.

Step 10: At the end of this period of writing, read over what you've written. Notice any ideas, symbols or patterns that have emerged. Use your writing to interpret them.

Calling S.O.S. to the Universe (technique 7)

When to use: when you are in a tight fix and need to manifest a solution to a problem or answers to a question fast.

Instructions:

Preparation:

Choose a time and place where you can write uninterrupted for as long as you need to finish writing the letter.

Take a plain sheet of paper and with pen in hand, just simply write.

Step one: "Dear Universe…"

Call out to the Universe. As you write, suspend any feelings of disbelief or doubt you might have as to whether this will work or not. Believe even for a moment that someone, something possessed of infinite wisdom, knowledge and power is reading your words as you write them.

Step two: "Here's my problem / situation…"

Describe your problem or situation generally. You don't have to go overboard in explaining all the minutest details involved in your problem or situation. But don't leave anything out.

Step three: "I am afraid that…"

Write to the Universe what it is that you fear about your situation. Explain your worries, doubts and concerns, and all that is making you anxious and stressed out about your problem. Don't hold back – if you want to describe the worst-case scenario (even if your rational mind tells you that it is not likely to happen), then do so.

Step four: "Here's what I want…"

Now tell the Universe exactly what you want. Describe everything that you want to have or happen in the minutest detail. This time, go overboard as much as you want. Give the Universe as many details as you want as to what you would now like to happen.

Step five: "Thank you for coming through for me."

Give thanks to the Universe for already fixing your issue or solving your problem for you, even when you see no evidence of it. Note any feelings of peace that you experience. You can also describe to the Universe the immense sense of relief that you now feel and thank it for handling this matter for you so completely and wonderfully.

Step six: "Now I let it go, become still and wait."

Sign your letter, put it in an envelope and seal it, or place it in a special box that you will now tuck away hidden from view. You have done everything you need to and can do. There is nothing else to be done. Again, allow yourself to be filled with immense relief and even joyous expectation knowing the solution to your problem is now on its way and it will not be a moment late.

Discernment of the Spirits (technique 10)

When to use: when needing to make an important decision and you want to be absolutely sure that it's the right one; to receive inner or supernatural guidance in decision making.

Instructions:

Preparation:
Understand the key points about the discernment process
First. Trust that guidance is available to you.
Second. Identify the discernment question.
Third. Know the facts and use your reason.
Fourth. Recognize your Consolations and Desolations.

WRITING TO RECEIVE ANSWERS

Fifth. Test the choices either in reality or in your imagination.

Sixth. Decide for one of the choices with time and in peace.

Discernment of the spirits:

7 steps of discernment

Remember to write everything that comes up through this process.

Step 1: Identify your true desires

Step 2: Use reason to weigh the options

Step 3: Consider or simulate the chosen option

Step 4: Weigh "consolations" versus "desolations"

Step 5: Subject the consolations to time and meditation

Step 6: Make the decision

WRITING TO INSPIRE

Gratitude Listing (technique 5)

When to use: to create your own miracle in 40 days; to learn the true value of gratitude and forgiveness in creating miracles and apply them.

Instructions:

Step 1: Commit to the process for at least 40 days.

Write down the starting and end dates on your journal, diary or calendar.

Step 2: Answer this question, "what do you want?"

Be specific in what you ask for. Write your request down. Even if the answer is obvious write it down anyway.

Step 3: Determine if you'll go through this process by yourself or with a partner.

Either way is equally effective and each one has its benefits and challenges.

Going through this process by yourself will be suitable if you've always preferred discovering things and gaining new knowledge alone.

If you decide to go through this process with a partner, choose someone you trust implicitly. Agree with your partner on some rules on how you will work together.

Step 4: Decide on a method of recording and communication.

Whether you're doing this technique alone or with a partner, choose a method for recording your lists; additionally, if doing with a partner, choose a method of communicating your lists to each other.

Step 5: Each morning or night, list what you are grateful for.

On your journal or blank document if you're using a word processor, write or type on top of the page, "today I am grateful for/that". Or if you prefer, you can also write, "Thank you for/that" and then write your list.

Step 6: For each item on your list, briefly state why you are grateful for it.

Step 7: List down the people you resent, who have wronged or offended you and who you can't forgive or haven't forgiven.

Vision Mapping (technique 8)

When to use: to create your true life vision and map out a clear, concise and direct course to that vision.

Instructions:

Step 1. Choose the area to envision

You can set a vision for all size projects and to suit every budget.

Step 2. Decide the timeline

You can set anything from two to 10-year visions, with 5 years being the typical period. But if you're new to envisioning, you can also start with a smaller one to 6-month project.

Step 3. Identify the milestones

Think about the ultimate result you want to achieve. What are the milestones that would have to be reached to build up to the big victorious result? Don't take too much time listing them – typically spend about 10 minutes. You can always add more later on.

Step 4. Write out your vision

Write out the first draft of your vision. You can start out by writing: "It's (put down the timeline you've decided on above). There are so many great things happening that make it clear that our long-term vision has become the reality that we hoped and believed it would back when we wrote it." Don't dwell too long on this step. Half an hour is a good amount of time to spend on it. Just keep writing until your time is up. Then forget about the draft for a few days or even longer as required by your project.

Step 5. Revise your vision

Read your first draft in its entirety. Pay close attention to what you wrote in that first draft. If you wrote honestly and from your core, the first draft will be the expression of your vision at its most authentic. For the succeeding drafts, aim for specificity. Be very specific and write in as many fine details as possible when revising your draft. Feel free to do further drafts if you feel like you have to, but a maximum of four redrafts is best.

Step 6. Get trusted feedback

This includes getting feedback from other decision-makers if you're not the only one and you're writing out an organizational vision. You also ask for feedback on your draft from those trusted others whose opinion you respect and value, but who are not necessarily insiders to the organization.

Step 7. Get hustling!

Now it's time to share your vision on a wholescale level – that is, with all those who will take part in executing it or will be affected by it.

Think, Write, Decree (technique 9)

When to use: to write your own personal declaration of accomplishment, victory or independence and command it to come to pass in your life.

Instructions:

Step 1: Write the Preamble.

- Why are you writing this declaration now?
- What is it that you want to happen as a result of making this declaration?
- What do you want to achieve?
- What do you want to declare independence from?
- Why do you want to achieve what you want to achieve?
- Why do you want to be free from whatever it is you seek independence from?

Step 2: List down your self-evident truths.

- Write down what you hold to be true about you, what you believe and hold sacred, and what you will always hold onto.
- List down your truths, the beliefs that you now choose to hold, regardless of what may happen around you or what other people say or believe about you, and in the face of all opposition from internal or external forces and despite all evidence to the contrary.

Step 3: Explain why you are left with no other recourse.

- Explain what will happen to you personally, and the people that you love, if your current condition, state of being, or undesirable circumstance were to persist.
- Describe what the price will be for you if things did not change.

Step 4: Now make your declarations.

- You can start by saying who you are. You can say your name, "Now, I, Jane or John Smith…".
- After your name, you might also add a descriptor of who you are or the person who you want to be or believe you are becoming. You can literally write any words here describing who you are or believe you are.
- State that you are making this with single-minded, unwavering, unflinching purpose.
- If you are making your declaration with other people, then state that you are doing this as a single united action.
- State in whose name you are doing this act.
- Then, actually state that you are making a solemn declaration, writing it down on paper and making it known to the whole world.
- Now list down your declarations. "I declare that from now on…" or "I declare that…"

- Write each declaration as a simple, single statement. Go straight to the point. Make it punchy.

Step 5: Finally, call on God's protection over your declaration.

- "And for the support of my declaration, firmly relying on divine providence," or other similar words.
- If you don't believe in God, but believe in some other power, then call on that power to protect your declaration.

Step 6: Write what you are giving in exchange for making this solemn covenant, this sacred contract.

- What is that thing that you are pledging and giving which gives substance to your contract or covenant?
- Write "I pledge my," or "we mutually pledge to each other," then write whatever it is that you are giving in exchange for this declaration.

Step 7: Sign your declaration.

- It is strongly recommended that you write out your declaration by hand, on paper, and sign it with your name and signature.
- It's also ok to type your declaration and print it out on paper. But you must sign it.

WRITING TO CHRONICLE

Creating solid self-confidence (technique 12)

When to use: when you need to create solid self-confidence and self-belief and develop resilience.

Instructions:

Write down your lifetime successes

Step 1: Take stock of the nine major, breakthrough successes you've experienced in your life.

Step 2: Divide your life up to this point into three equal periods. For example:

Your age: 42

- First third of my life: birth to age 14
- Second third of my life: age 15 to 28
- Third stage of my life: age 29 to present

Another example: if you're 27 years old –

- First third of my life: birth to age 9
- Second third of my life: age 10 to 19
- Third stage of my life: age 20 to present

Step 3: For each time period, write down the three major successes you've experienced. List down what you feel is a win or a successful, victorious outcome.

Three things you did well today

Step 1: Every night, before you retire, set aside 10 to 15 minutes.

Step 2: Take out your journal or notebook.

Step 3: Write down the three things you did well that day. Again, as with the above technique, it doesn't matter whether what you did well that day is small or big, major or minor.

Daily win log

Step 1: Write down all your wins for the day.

Step 2: Write down how and why you are grateful for each one of them.

Step 3: Do this technique mindfully.

- Relive the feelings of victory you felt when you scored these successes.
- When you do appreciation writing, feel truly grateful and overjoyed at the things you appreciate in your life.

My 101 lifetime successes

Preparation:

Before you start this technique, remind yourself that you are already a winner and that you are continuing to win in life. You can write this out as a short statement and write it at the start of your list.

Step 1: Divide your life into about 5 or 6 periods and then write about 15 to 20 successes for each period.

- If it makes it easier, write the date or at least the year when you experienced this victory.

Step 2: After each item, write a statement to remind yourself how much of a winner and a victor you are.

- For example: "I am successful", "I am accomplished"; "I am distinguished"; "I can do great things"; "I am respected and accomplished".

Step 3: As you write each item, try to recall the feelings of winning and success that you felt when you achieved those victories.

- Relish and savor the delicious feelings and sensations you felt at each of those moments.
- And as you do so, remind yourself of a simple truth: "I am already a winner!"

Step 4: List down your wins, both spectacular and humble, big and small.

Step 5: Finish your list and write your 101st success or victory

Step 6: Read over your list of victories from time to time.

- As you do, remind yourself constantly that you are already greatly successful, that you are victorious in life.
- Acknowledge that that there will be countless other victories, wins and breakthroughs waiting for you in the future.

WRITING TO CHRONICLE

Charting Your Hero's Journey (technique 13)

When to use: when needing guidance in life from patterns of the universal human story; when you want to prove that you are an everyday hero.

Instructions:

Preparation: read the positive statements below, which briefly describe each stage of the hero's journey. Then think about the questions under each stage of the hero's journey. Reflect and write your answers in your journal. If you come to other realizations as you reflect on each stage, then write those down too.

Stage 1: The Ordinary World

Before I can enter a higher level of life, I must first live in the ordinary world. Apart from my actual environment, the ordinary world can also represent my comfort zone, conditioned beliefs and behaviors.

- What does the ordinary world look like for me?
- What is my current comfort zone?
- Do I feel like I'm going through my current life in a daze, like I am just going through the motions of living?
- Am I living my life bored, listless, without any passion or excitement?

Stage 2: My Call to Adventure

The Call to Adventure is a call for me to leave the ordinary world and travel to a special one, a world in which I will be actualizing all my potential as a person, and using my gifts and talents to become the best version of myself and serve humanity and the world.

- Do I feel an urge to do something out of the ordinary in my life? In my work? In my relationships? In my living arrangements?

- Do I sense that I need to change something in my life or the way I've been living it?

- Is there something I know I must do that will serve my highest good as a person, but which I am resisting?

- Is there an important decision that could potentially change my life (and by extension my family's life) for the better, which I am afraid to make or am putting off?

- Do I feel the need to get out of my comfort zone and venture into an unknown, but exciting, future?

- Do I have a grand vision for my life, in which I am existing as the best possible version of myself, in which the different areas of my life have reached their highest levels?

- Is there something that my heart is pulling me to do but which my brain is discouraging me from doing because it's unrealistic, impractical or will never work?

Stage 3: Meeting my Mentors

At one point in my quest, someone unexpectedly comes along offering me aid, assistance or encouragement that could help me travel farther or overcome the challenges and obstacles blocking my path. I don't know when the mentor will appear but I have faith that he or she will come when I am ready.

- Are there any people in my life right now who know the mission I've decided to take and are already helping me in some way to succeed in it?

- Am I accepting or refusing their offer of aid?

- Who are the people whose help, knowledge, wisdom, talents, skills or resources I will need to help me achieve my goals?

- If a potential mentor is present, what actions can I take to get them to know and help me?

- Can I seek help, wisdom or advice from my higher self or inner guidance system?

Stage 4: Crossing the First Threshold

Once I go through the first door or cross the first bridge, it bursts into flames. I cannot turn back, at least not the way by which I came.

- What major decision can I make right now that would represent the first step out of my comfort zone and toward my envisioned life?

- What one powerful action can I take right now that would show that I am committed to moving toward my big goals?

- What one act am I afraid or even terrified of doing but which I know, if I did it, will represent a breakthrough in my life and in my goals?

Stage 5: My Road of Trials

Along my hero's journey, I expect to encounter many obstacles and challenges. I anticipate facing many foes, whether human, material, situational or circumstantial, all intent on stopping me from completing my journey and finding my treasure. This comes as no surprise. I expect this because I acknowledge that adversity is how the universe tests my commitment to succeed in my journey.

- What obstacles lie between me and the higher vision I have seen for my life?
- What challenges are hindering me from taking further steps toward my goals?
- Are there people who are trying to stop me from moving forward in my quest?
- Are there any circumstances, situations, conditions or factors that are making it difficult for me to continue moving toward my goals?

Stage 6: The Dragon's Den

The next threshold is often more challenging or treacherous than the first. This could involve a second major decision that I take along my hero's journey; it could put me at significant physical and psychological risk. But I also realize that within the walls of my darkest, innermost cave also lies the cornerstone of the special world I am trying to reach. I know that my goal is within reach.

- Are there signs that my goal or objective is now coming closer to me?
- Do things feel more difficult now that I can see my goal?

- What challenges or obstacles am I facing right now that are hindering me from achieving my ultimate objective?

- Am I tempted to give in to despair and lose hope, abandon my quest and give up?

Stage 7: My Moment of Despair

I know that the journey toward my ultimate goal is an adventure. And no adventure worth taking is ever easy. I realize that there are many dangers that lie before me on the path to self-realization and self-discovery. I must not give up and lose hope, knowing that success is assured as long as I persevere toward my ultimate goal.

- Does it seem like nothing is happening and that I'm not getting any closer to my goal or objective?

- Am I now doubting that I can succeed in my quest and achieve my ultimate goal?

- Am I faced with a major obstacle that is making my immediate future look dark?

- Does it look like I'm stuck in a trap, that mentally I cannot see a way ahead, and that I'm about to lose my way, my self or my values in my quest toward my goal?

- Can I draw on resources, both internal (my hidden reserves of energy, strength, faith, industry and creativity) and external (other people, my own support networks), to help me survive this ordeal and successfully emerge from the cave?

Stage 8: Attaining the Ultimate Prize

I have now overcome my major obstacles and emerged from my dark cave of doubt and despair. I have successfully achieved my ultimate goal. I have attained my desire. I have reached the end of my journey and arrived at my destination. While I may have obtained the prize, I realize that the real reward is my own inner transformation.

- How have I changed as a person by having completed my quest and achieved my goals?

- What are the valuable lessons I have learned during this process?

- Do I feel an obligation to share what I have learned with others, to help them on their own hero's journey?

- What am I impelled to do now that I have been successful in my quest?

Stage 9: Returning with the Prize

I acknowledge that my entire life is one big adventure, an unending quest to realize my highest self and be the best version of myself. There will always be challenges ahead of me, both physical, psychological, mental and even spiritual. I am determined to overcome all these challenges. I also recognize that there will be future calls to adventure and further journeys for me to embark on.

- What new challenges or roadblocks still lie in front of me as I make my way back after achieving my goal?

- After I have completed my hero's journey, are there any unresolved issues that I must now face and resolve?

- After gaining valuable lessons from my quest, am I being called to share my newfound knowledge to serve humanity and the world?

- Can I identify personal areas of weakness that I must improve if I am to become the best possible version of myself?

Stage 10: Looking back from a higher level

Before coming home with my new-found wisdom, there is often one more unforeseen challenge. This trial could be the most difficult of them all; it is a test that I must pass to cement my personal transformation.

- What unsuspected ordeal has now emerged after I have achieved my ultimate goal?

- What new knowledge and skills have I gained from my quest that I can now use to overcome this final hurdle?

- Do I feel more confident that I am able to handle the demands brought about by my new life?

www.ingramcontent.com/pod-product-compliance
Lightning Source LLC
Chambersburg PA
CBHW021356290426
44108CB00010B/270